3/

PELICAN BOOKS

MARITAL BREAKDOWN

Jack Dominian, who was born in Athens in 1929, left Greece in 1941 and completed his education in Bombay and in England. He qualified as a doctor in 1955 after training at Fitzwilliam House, Cambridge, and the Radcliffe Infirmary, Oxford, and in 1961 he qualified as a psychiatrist. After seven years at the Maudsley Hospital he left it in 1965 to take up his present position as head of the Department of Psychological Medicine at the Central Middlesex Hospital; he is also consultant psychiatrist at Shenley Hospital. Since 1958 he has been a medical adviser to the Catholic Marriage Advisory Council, particularly concerned with the challenge that modern psychiatry and psychology present to traditional Christian thinking.

His published investigations cover a wide range of psychiatric subjects, and he has written many articles. He is also the author of *Psychiatry and the Christian* (1962), *Christian Marriage, the Challenge of Change* (1967) and *The Church and the Sexual Revolution* (1971). He also edits and contributes to a forthcoming book, *The New Poor*.

Dr Dominian is married and has four children.

JACK DOMINIAN

MARITAL BREAKDOWN

PENGUIN BOOKS

Penguin Books Ltd, Harmondsworth, Middlesex, England
Penguin Books Inc., 7110 Ambasador Road, Baltimore, Maryland, 21207, U.S.A.
Penguin Books Australia Ltd, Ringwood, Victoria, Australia

—

First published by Penguin Books and Darton, Longman & Todd 1968
Reprinted in Penguin Books 1969, 1971, 1974

—

Made and printed in Great Britain by
Hazell Watson & Viney Ltd, Aylesbury, Bucks
Set in Linotype Times

—

Library edition available from Darton, Longman & Todd Ltd

CONTENTS

PREFACE

THE scientific study of marriage began at the turn of the century and has been gathering momentum with each succeeding decade. The United States has taken a lead in this research first through sociology and later with a psychological approach. This book gives a selected survey of this research both in the United States and Britain, to which I have added my own observations, based on ten years' work in this field. Research into marriage is difficult, not only by virtue of the complexity of the subject itself but because matrimony stands at the centre of powerful social, religious and legal ordinances which influence this most intimate of personal relationships in different ways.

However daunting the difficulties may appear, there is an urgent need to overcome them, for the plight of marriage concerns everyone, the sufferers, their off-spring and society as a whole. Different religious and ethical backgrounds may divide men and women in the proposed solutions *after* a marriage breaks down, but there is little disagreement about the desirability of identifying and rectifying the causes *before* this happens.

Two subjects, alcoholism and sexual deviation, have not been treated in detail in this book because they are the themes of separate Pelican books in the Studies in Social Pathology Series.

I want to record my particular appreciation to the publishers for their continuous support and help throughout all stages of preparing this book. My sincere thanks are also due to Professor G. M. Carstairs, Professor D. Pond and Dr. D. Bardon who gave generously of their time and advice.

I also wish to express my debt to the various authors and publishers upon whose works and articles I have drawn. All of them are mentioned in the references which provide a guide for further reading. In particular my appreciation is due to the following authors and publishers for permission to quote from their studies: E. W. Burgess and P. Wallin, and J. B. Lippincott Co.; Dr E. Slater and M. Woodside, and Cassell & Co. Ltd.; R. F. Winch, R. McGinnis and H. R. Barringer, and Holt, Rinehart and Winston Inc.; W. J. Goode and Prentice-Hall Inc., Population Studies, for permission to reproduce Table 5; and Acta Psychiatrica Scandinavica for permission to reproduce Table 4.

ONE

CONTEMPORARY MARRIAGE

THE subject of marital failure is neither new nor peculiar to our age. The breakdown of marriage with provisions for divorce and remarriage is a phenomenon widely recognized in Babylonian, Hebrew, Greek and Roman law. Christianity established a new ideal of life-long indissoluble marriage in Europe and in those parts of the world where western civilization has had an influence. But in the last three hundred years and particularly during the last century there has been a gradual lessening of Christian influence and the emergence of civic codes based on secular philosophies. So the earlier solutions have been re-introduced. Divorce is thus a return to a pre-Christian solution to marital failure.

Marital failure is the breakdown of a human relationship, an event before which societies have hitherto remained passive, perplexed and rather helpless witnesses. This is now beginning to change. The sciences of sociology and psychology are bringing this subject within the orbit of their research and already valuable insights are emerging which with the passage of time could lead to effective intervention, prophylactically and therapeutically. Such an approach begs the question whether intervention is desirable, but if the answer is in the affirmative and this appears to correspond to the view of Christian and humanist thinking, then we shall be turning to these sciences increasingly for the solution of an age-long baffling problem.

In this opening Chapter a short summary is given of the recent evolution of marriage in order to outline the background against which the sociological and psychological findings can be evaluated.

Until the industrial revolution marriage and the family formed a cohesive unit centred on the home which was the site of both production and consumption. In a predominantly agricultural economy a large part of the manufacture of goods was organized in the home where the spouses and the children contributed their skills and energies. The advent of the factory as the centre of production brought about a permanent separation of home and work for the husband. Later, married women became similarly engaged outside the home except for those periods when pregnancy and the rearing of children kept them at home. These changes have exposed the members of the family on the one hand to the benefits of outside influences and on the other to the stresses of coping with these new environmental demands. Whatever the difficulties there is no return to the restrictive safety and isolation of former times.

The home has not only lost its manufacturing value but the arrival of the powerful modern state has also divested it of other essential functions. Of these education is a good example. Its formal components take place entirely outside the home while the trend of extending infant and nursery schooling is likely to relieve the mother of further responsibility at an earlier age. The advances of medicine have reduced the incidence of childhood illnesses and the acute phases of disease are handled in the hospital, further freeing the members of a family from time-consuming responsibilities. Finally in recent decades economic measures have been taken to support the family in time of stress by providing security during sickness and relieving the anxiety associated with unemployment and old age. Collectively these measures have released talents and energies which have to be redeployed.

The reorganization consequent to these social changes has coincided with the breakdown of the patriarchal system which invested overwhelming power and authority in the hands of the male head of the family. The removal of the father from home to the factory and the reduction of the tasks for which he was responsible undoubtedly contributed to this change. But an even bigger influence has been the gradual emancipation of woman from being man's appointed vassal to a status not far short of his own. In the presence of increasing awareness of the significance of the individual the two World Wars largely contributed to the breakdown of the antifeminine bias. It was sharply realized that there was little men could do which women could not do as well, and the hitherto accepted distinctions were more often than not exclusiveness due to ignorance and prejudice. Psychology added yet another mortal blow by showing undeniably that there were no overall intelligence differences between the sexes and that indeed in some areas women were more proficient. These insights would have been of little value, however, unless women were able to secure economic independence. We have still not reached the position of complete equality of financial reward for equal work but this is a goal which is being approached. The progress already made has produced sufficient economic independence to introduce yet another permanent factor in the relationship between the sexes.

Social changes brought about by the industrial revolution, the intervention of the state, and the most important single event, the emancipation of women, have allowed modern marriage to be seen more as a companionship than as an institution brought about and regulated by a legal contract. Marriage experienced in this way is veering away from the framework of mutual duties and rights towards the highest possible satisfaction of personal needs. It is thus becoming increasingly recognized and examined in terms of a personal relationship in which mutual needs are fulfilled in the complementarity of the sexes. There are many aspects of this relationship – physical, psychological, social and spiritual, – each taking a particular significance in the various stages of courtship and the marriage itself.

Courtship and the selection of the partner have altered in three ways. The young man and woman are now the principal agents concerned with the seeking and accepting of each other as husband and wife. Parents and relations usually provide a welcome confirmation of the selection but are no longer the influential agents who direct the operation. Arranged marriages are almost completely superseded by personal selection which is now based on romantic love. 'By romantic love, we understand an engrossing emotional attachment between a man and a woman, exclusive and individualized, transcending at need all sorts of obstacles, involving some kind of idealization, and enveloping the sex relationship in an aura of tender sentiment for the personality of the loved one.'[1]

This engrossing emotional attachment is very much in evidence as the contemporary ideal depicted in all forms of modern art and translated to a varying degree in every courtship. Romantic love first appears as a significant element in the thirteenth century amongst the troubadours. It was based on an idealization of the woman and the extolling of love outside marriage. The idealization remains but the goal has been changed and it is contractual marriage that has now become the vehicle of this exclusive personal devotion. Harmonizing romantic love within life-long monogamy is one of the many challenges offered to contemporary marriage.

Marriage is thus stripped of previous duties and is free to concentrate on three age-old human needs and one new one. These are the satisfaction of sexual needs, the procreation and the rearing of children, and the setting up of a home. The new emphasis resulting from the release from other responsibilities is on the personal development of the spouses. Such an orientation naturally places a great deal more importance on the capacity of the partners to meet these more complex conscious and unconscious aspirations in personal relationships.

During the last few decades there has been a particular preoccupation with two aspects of this personal relationship, namely sexual fulfilment and the size of the family. Despite the widespread attention that these subjects have attracted, it is fair to say that, like divorce, they are not new topics. The history of ancient civilization was marked by a preoccupation with the tensions between the erotic and the social, procreative aspects of marriage. Except in the case of the ban on divorce, the impact of Christianity in this sphere is not easy to evaluate. It must certainly take a considerable share of responsibility for the devaluation of sexual values but there have been non-Christian sources at work as well. This subject still awaits a comprehensive examination. Whatever the answer, a number of new factors have combined to bring the subject into prominence. The principal ones have been the emancipation of woman, the impact of Freudian psychology and the advance of utilitarian philosophies opposed to Christian asceticism.

The combination of these forces, aided by modern researches, has produced a climate of opinion in which sexual relations have assumed a central significance. It is now accepted that woman has the same right to enjoy her sexual life as man and, since there are biological and psychological handicaps which belong to her alone, special attention has been directed to helping her to understand her own sexuality. Man also needs to understand woman's complex sexual response and to learn to adapt his own sexuality to meet her needs.

These advances have been facilitated by the widespread use of effective methods controlling procreation. In the richness of material that will confront the social historian of the future, the development of birth regulation will play a large and important part. Birth regulation has not only permitted the restriction of families to the required size, but has undoubtedly confronted couples with a deeper and wider involvement of their sexuality.

Birth regulation coupled with advanced medicine is making increasingly possible a very desirable objective. The time is approaching when children will only be conceived when their parents want them and are able to give them the unconditional care and love which is such a necessary pre-requisite for the development of their health physically and psychologically. The gains in physical health are already fairly obvious. The implementation of psychological research, being a much more complicated subject, is naturally lagging behind but some of the newly released time and energy of the parents is likely to find its way in developing new ways of safeguarding the integrity of the personality in childhood on which so much depends for the future welfare of the individual.

This brief outline of modern marriage contains the clues to some of the vulnerable elements leading to instability. There is one overall concern permeating every aspect of the relationship, namely the determined effort to seek and attain a high degree of personal fulfilment. The material expectations are relatively easy to fulfil in a buoyant, economically advancing society; the emotional and spiritual ones depend almost entirely on the resources of the individual in a home situation which is frequently distant from the support and the help of the other members of the family.

The fostering of egalitarian relationships between the spouses and between spouses and children permits bonds which are based on the value of personal worth rather than on the arbitrary basis of fear and authority. These structured hierarchical relationships were undoubtedly restricting but had the advantage of stability, continuity and little need for invention. There is security in conformity. Equality requires constant adaptation so that personal rights and status are safeguarded and feelings not hurt. To achieve this in the ever changing complexity of roles within marriage requires personalities who are adaptive, flexible and stable, to accommodate each other without compromise or damage. When these qualities are absent there will be ambiguity, confusion, disappointment, difficulties in communication and much misunderstanding. Furthermore, disappointments and frustrations from this or any other cause cannot be easily unloaded on to readily receptive and sympathetic members of the parental home. They have to be carried within the individual. Isolation and the danger of mounting stress is all too common a phenomenon.

Modern marriage is committed to the goals of independence, freedom and the attainment of the highest possible standards of personal fulfilment. Since the welfare of societies and nations depends on the well-being of the individual marriage and family, we have to learn how best they can be achieved. It can only be done by widespread education and preparation for marriage, the identification through research of its intrinsic destructive forces, and the provision of readily available and effective help for those who need it.

TWO

THE INCIDENCE AND TIMING OF MARITAL BREAKDOWN

MARRIAGE in western societies has been considered throughout the centuries as a solemn, life-long contract between a man and a woman, conferring mutual rights and obligations in their sexual, material and social life. The specific or primary purpose for such a union has always been the procreation and rearing of children. Marriage has been dealt with almost exclusively in these legal terms, the law defining the formal conditions which bring such a unique institution into being and similarly when it has failed prescribing the conditions under which it can be dissolved.

While the law of the land can set up clearly the conditions under which a valid marriage can be entered into or dissolved, such a purely legal framework cannot say much that is useful about the nature of marriage. It can only erect precise limits to its origin and conclusion, in the name of society. Marriage seen in these contractual terms is brought about through a formal commitment but its essence is a viable relationship between the spouses spanning many decades. This relationship between the spouses themselves and their children is subjected to the constant fluctuations of physical and mental health as well as a variety of social pressures. Such a complex situation is bound to experience friction, conflict and some discontent as part of its very existence.

A study by Pierce [2] examined some of the difficulties facing couples who married in the fifties in England and Wales. Adjustment difficulties were reported in 48·2 per cent of the sample interviewed, which covered a cross-section of the community marrying during these years. This high incidence included a wide range of problems associated with housing, money, family and in-laws, religion and sexual difficulties, and is no measure of an ultimate serious breakdown. It is the extension of such conflicts to a wider, deeper and more continuous failure to meet and satisfy each other's essential needs that leads to marital failure. In this chapter marital breakdown will be considered in terms of the ultimate separation of the couple with or without divorce. Figures are only available for this ultimate breakdown but neither separation nor divorce is an accurate gauge for marital breakdown for this term also comprises couples who continue to live under the same roof but have ceased to have a marital relationship. This means that the available figures have to be interpreted with caution and would tend to under-estimate the total size of the problem. The rise of divorce was at first slow but it has become rapid in the last few decades. From 1715 to 1852 the average number of divorces was less than two a year. Currently they fluctuate round about the 30,000 mark annually. Absolute numbers, however, are misleading. The married population has increased at least three times since 1857, life expectation is greater and the figures for any one year may not reflect accurately a trend but relate to some specific event causing a temporary upsurge. There was an increase in the number of divorces granted after both world wars, after the Matrimonial Causes Act of 1937, after the extension of financial relief with the Poor Person's procedure in 1914 and 1920, and again in 1949 with legal aid. It is more useful and accurate to describe the increase in terms of rates and incidence.

Rowntree and Carrier,[3] in their extensive studies of divorce in England and Wales, give a very clear-cut account of the rise in the petitions filed per 10,000 of married women aged fifteen to forty-nine. This rate was 0·83 in the period 1861–65, 9·46 in 1919, 15·86 in 1938, 50·0 in 1948 and after a further rise slightly declined in 1956 to 54·6, the last year for which figures are given. It is calculated that from the 1861–65 period to 1937 the divorce rate increased by 319 per cent and that the Second World War was associated with a further increase of 337 per cent. There is no suggestion as yet that these large increases are temporary effects resulting from the Second World War.

Divorce is a clearly defined event describing the termination of the marriage contract and as such lends itself to fairly accurate measurement. As an index of marital breakdown it portrays, however, only part of the total picture, which includes temporary and permanent separations as well as acute and protracted suffering while the spouses continue to cohabit. Rowntree [4] has extended her studies to give a more accurate analysis by including some of these couples. She based her results on a national sample of 3,000 men and women between the ages of 16 and 59 who were questioned in 1960 and whose marriages covered the years 1930 to 1949. Tracing successive groups who were married between 1930 and 1949, she found that up to 1960 some six to ten per cent had experienced an episode of separation of which five to seven per cent had terminated in divorce. Two to four per cent had contemplated separation. *Thus between 8 and 14 per cent of the informants admitted to marital problems severe enough to contemplate separation, actually experience it or end in divorce.* These figures suggest that the initial high incidence of adjustment difficulties, estimated to occur in nearly 50 per cent of marriages, was resolved for the vast majority of the couples. There remains a small but not insignificant percentage for whom marriage is unworkable with their original partner.

Figures from the United States of America, as indeed for all countries in which civil divorce is permitted, confirm the upward trend. Jacobson [5] covers the period 1860 to 1956 in the United States. During this time the divorce rate rose and, after a sharp increase following the Second World War, settled down to a rate eight times higher than in 1860. He estimated that the proportion of newly-weds who ended in divorce in 1950 was around 17 per cent. This is approximately twice the rate found in Britain but the methods of computation make exact comparisons difficult. It is interesting that marriages broken by death of the spouse were reduced by more than a third during the same period. The giant strides made by the medical sciences to preserve and sustain life have had no beneficial effect on the stability of marriage; in fact, some dissolutions, which are now occurring in the civil courts, might have been anticipated in an earlier period by the death of one of the spouses.

Divorce can take place at any phase in the course of a marriage subject to the legal requirements of the country concerned. Couples may terminate their relationship soon after marriage begins, after the children have arrived or when they have grown up and many years of marriage have elapsed. In Britain divorce proceedings may not be started during the first three years of marriage except in very special circumstances.

Several studies have examined the *duration* of marriage prior to divorce. Monahan and Chancellor[6] found this to be between six and ten years in the State of Iowa in the United States; similar findings were recorded by Hill and Tarver[7] in the State of Wisconsin, and Goode[8] in his study of 425 divorced women records an average period of 8·7 years. A more extensive study of divorces in Sweden, analysing the annual risk of divorce up to forty years after marriage shows that divorce increases from the time of marriage reaching a maximum about four years later.[9] An analysis of the 32,052 divorces and annulments granted in 1963 in England and Wales shows that the dissolutions reach a peak six to seven years after the start of the marriage.[10] These statistics differ somewhat, but they are all in agreement that divorce has a high incidence in the early years of marriage, which appears to be the critical phase. These figures, however, are deceptive and not a reliable guide to the development and natural course of severe marital disharmony. The average years referred to are determined by a number of factors such as the laws relating to the period after the ceremony prior to the permissible beginning of proceedings and the variable duration of these. A more accurate picture can be gained by studying not the years prior to divorce but the time before the couple separate. This is, in fact, the operative time when the home is disrupted by the spouses living apart. Monahan[11] summarizes thc findings of various investigators and describes his own findings based on 4,282 divorce actions, the number registered in the year 1957 in Wisconsin, U.S.A. He shows that the period elapsing between separation and divorce ranges from two to five years. His own findings were that the first year of marriage shows the highest incidence of separation, with the second as the next highest. His results strongly suggest a tendency for early marital disruption, much earlier than the divorce statistics suggest. These studies, whose findings place the most vulnerable phase of marriage in the first two or three years of marriage, need to be repeated in several countries. If confirmed, they will prove of the greatest importance by pinpointing a phase which needs the maximum assistance.

Although the early years show the highest incidence of breakdown, divorce continues and marriages break down after thirty years or more of matrimony. It is unlikely that the same disintegrative mechanisms operate throughout all these years. At this stage of research the causal factors and the way they operate are only just beginning to be elucidated but evidence will be presented throughout the book which will place the primary responsibility in the personality of the spouses and the specific interaction of the couple.

The statistics nevertheless indicate that marital breakdown can be divided broadly into at least two phases. The first one spans approximately the first five years of marriage during which breakdown is brought about by the failure to establish the necessary minimum relationship physically and emotionally. Marriages which negotiate this phase with reasonable success enter into a second phase in which the relationship is subjected to different stresses. These are complex and as yet ill understood but recent research points to several factors.

One of these is the inevitable maturation of the personality with the passage of time. New traits and needs attain prominence which are no longer recognized or met by the partner. The earlier the marriage starts the greater are the likely changes in the personality requiring considerable mutual adaptation later on. One reason for the high incidence of divorce in youthful marriages is precisely this marked change which exposes the couple to completely new facets of themselves. Another factor which is emerging from the research of the last twenty years suggests that in this second phase the couple achieve an emotional closeness which induces a return of an earlier situation in which unresolved emotional difficulties with parental figures are relived, the place of the unsatisfactory parent being taken by the spouse. Finally the marriage experiences a new situation when the children are grown up and leave the home, exposing both parents, but particularly the mother, to the challenge of redirecting their emotional and social life. These and other factors will be discussed in later chapters. If later research confirms these critical phases and the factors mentioned, it will make the task of prevention and reconciliation easier by encouraging couples to seek help earlier and by concentrating therapy on the crucial points.

THREE

CHOOSING A PARTNER: SOCIAL AND RELIGIOUS FACTORS

THE systematic examination of marriage and the family was first undertaken by sociologists, who applied modern scientific methods in their studies from the thirties onwards. A central theme that runs through all the early research has been the attempt to identify the *social* factors that influence the choice of a partner. Later on psychologists and psychiatrists began to examine the psychological factors that determine selection and this stage of research is still in its early phase. The social criteria examined were the availability of equal numbers of men and women, their proximity to one another, the average age of marriage, their religious affiliation, social class, race and ethnic background. Extensive studies were carried out in the forties and fifties particularly in the United States and the results have established clearly that as far as these factors are concerned the process of selection is *homogamous*, that is to say like chooses like. This tendency for men and women to choose in each other characteristics similar to their own has been defined as *assortative mating*.

Social custom has changed considerably in the patterns of meeting, dating and courting. Within the space of a few decades young people of all social classes have developed habits which are markedly different from those of one or two generations ago. Principal amongst these is the waning influence of parents and relatives who are no longer in a position to arrange, strictly vet and effectively disapprove if necessary. The stringent interrogation of the handbag scene in Wilde's *The Importance of Being Earnest* is an event of history. It is broadly accepted that the choice of the future partner is the primary concern of the participants themselves. The approval of the parents may or may not be sought, although it is frequently welcomed when received. Even though parental opposition may still dissuade some individuals or delay the event for others, it does not constitute an insurmountable obstacle. This is an extension of freedom, which applies equally to men and women and Parliament is now considering the Latey Report which recommends that young people be allowed to marry at eighteen without parental consent.

At the same time as the influence of the parents has receded, the restrictions imposed on the permissible circle of friends have been greatly relaxed. The change from an agricultural to a predominantly industrial nation has shifted the emphasis from the village or small town to the big amorphous towns and cities where anonymity safeguards a wide range of experimentation with different associates. Modern transport, particularly the car, has made it possible to extend the area of contact, and the separation of the place of work from home, especially in the big cities, has added a new dimension to the range of possible choice. Altogether these changes have undoubtedly widened the range of possible contact but despite these alterations the immediate neighbourhood has not been ousted as the most likely meeting place for one's future partner.

Studies of engaged and married couples, whose place of residence was checked in the licence applications, have shown a large proportion of marriages still taking place between persons living very near to each other. This feature has been called *residential propinquity*, and two studies [12] in the United States have confirmed that approximately fifty per cent of the couples who met, dated and ultimately married, lived within thirteen or fewer standard blocks of each other.

Residential propinquity would naturally operate in favour of bringing together people of similar social background. Notwithstanding the increased freedom of choice available to the young, unhindered by parental control, extensive studies both in Britain and the United States show conclusively that the majority of couples marry *within their own social class*. One of the most detailed and extensive studies [13] carried out on the social characteristics of married couples was completed in New Haven, Connecticut, U.S.A. The marriage licence data of the 2,063 couples married in 1948 were examined. Social class similarity was confirmed. As might be expected *race and ethnic* backgrounds were also important. Hollingshead stresses this by not finding a single inter-racial marriage in his group. He writes: 'Our data suggest that the racial *mores* place the strongest, most explicit and most precise limits on an individual as to whom he may or may not marry.' The author is here expressing a point of view strongly influenced not only by his findings but by the special conditions of race relations in the United States. How long this powerful prohibition will continue to operate is a matter of conjecture but it undoubtedly exists, even though it is more pronounced in some parts of the world. Violation of such a norm carries distinct social risks and requires above average maturity and stability to withstand the censure of society. When such marriages are entered into impulsively or dictated by unrecognized emotional conflict, they carry an extra risk of breakdown, threatened as they are both by the hostility of society and the intrinsic vulnerability of the couple.

Within this broad similarity of social class and race, there were sub-groups showing variations. On the few occasions when the social class boundaries were crossed, it was the man who married a woman of lower and, at times, much lower social class. The reverse rarely took place. This finding is strikingly confirmed in an even larger study in Britain [14] in which 4,858 marriages covering all the main social classes were studied. Similarity of social class was broadly established. In 315 instances the man married a woman of lower social and educational background, the reverse being found in only 134 marriages.

These marriages, in which one spouse marries in a social class well below their own, are of special interest for marital breakdown. The motives behind such a marked transgression of social norms are frequently psychological in nature. Strong feelings of inadequacy, which may be conscious or unconscious, or a strong urge to assert independence and defy parental direction may persist long after the immediate defeat of the elders or the satisfaction of having obtained a spouse at last. These tendencies may exert corrosive influences on the marriage. The disharmony that follows is often confused by the inevitable temptation to put the whole blame on the social differences of customs, education, outlook and values. As in all marriages where social differences exist, it is important to separate these from the emotional influences and assist the couple in assessing the relative significance of each in their lives.

The number of marriages affected by marked social class differences are few, contributing very little to the total number of breakdowns. Greater attention has been paid to the relationship between social class itself and breakdown. This feature has been exhaustively examined in the United States, and particularly from the census of 1950.[15] Men and women, white and Negro, were separately assessed. One finding emerged with absolute consistency. As far as the white men were concerned, there was an inverse relationship between breakdown and income levels, educational background and occupational status. The lower levels in each category were associated with the highest incidence of separation and divorce. The relative immunity of the upper socio-economic group is explained by the hypothesis that there are more 'external supports' in these. Amongst these external supports Goode lists a greater continuity of social relations, more long-term material and social investments, greater difference between the husband's and the wife's earning power and less anonymity in the event of a marital rupture.[16]

Few comparable studies exist in Britain. Rowntree and Carrier [3] who studied the rate and characteristics of divorce in England and Wales during 1858–1957 could not confirm the findings in the United States and no significant relationship was found between occupation and divorce. Further detailed enquiries are warranted on this subject.

The American results are, nonetheless, so uniform that it is worth considering at least one of the reasons for this relationship. The occupation of a man is related to his intelligence, drive and stability in mastering and sustaining particular skills, professional, technical or manual. There is ample psychiatric evidence indicating that, in addition, a poor work record, as shown either by the frequency of change or the failure to attain a post commensurate to the individual's potential, is connected with marked psychological disorders. It may well be that the ranks of unskilled workers and the workless contain an excess of these individuals, who, as a result of their personal defects, can attain little other than menial work. There is supporting evidence for this view from the results of a detailed study of 425 divorces in the United States in which Goode [8] found that many divorced husbands had an unsteady work record.

Another important social factor that has also been studied extensively in the United States is the impact of religion on marital stability. Since Christianity with its strict teaching on divorce is the principal faith of western culture, its influence is considerable, although it is bound to vary, depending on the zeal of adherence to its tenets. This can of course vary from being merely a nominal to an extremely committed adherence. The investigations relating to religion have examined the type of ceremony, whether civil or religious, the denomination of the spouses and the effect of mixed religious affiliations on the marriage.

With regard to the ceremony itself, American studies tend to suggest that weddings with a civil ceremony alone run a higher risk of breakdown than those carried out in a church. But a detailed review of cases referred to the National Marriage Guidance Council in Britain does not confirm this finding.[17] The proportion of civilly married couples among these cases was no greater than the average for the country. The objection here is that these marriages are not necessarily a representative sample of all marriages that break down. Further studies are needed to assess this factor and compare the findings between the two countries.

Even if the American results are confirmed, the significance of this finding has to be cautiously interpreted. It is true that a civil contract does not carry for the partners the absolute prohibition of divorce present in the Christian faith. It could thus be argued that couples starting their married life under the auspices of a religious ceremony receive an inbuilt advantage. But what is the nature of this advantage? It should be remembered that even in the Roman Catholic Church, which considers a marriage between two baptised Christians a sacrament, the sacramental state does not result from the presence of the couple in the church, nor that of the priest, but from the exchange of the vows and the acceptance of the commitments involved. The motivation and determination derived from faith is infinitely more important than the outward manifestations and place of the ceremony. Furthermore civil weddings will have a higher proportion of hurried marriages, of those facing parental opposition and of those likely to belong to the younger age group, all of which place them in the higher bracket of vulnerability. If these factors were eliminated, it is possible that the association would not be found, but this will have to await further research.

Most religious denominations actively encourage marriage between members of their own faith. Thus religion joins social class as a restrictive influence on the choice of partner. The rate of *intrafaith* marriages depends, of course, on the availability of equal proportions of men and women of the same denomination. Data on a national scale both from Canada and the United States, have shown that the inter-denominational marriages increase as the proportion of a particular religious group in the population decreases.

Mixed marriages have been and continue to be condemned with particular vigour by Judaism and Roman Catholicism. Do the results of these marriages warrant these severe warnings? The conclusion of all major studies appears to indicate that mixed marriages, especially when they involve a Roman Catholic and another denomination, do run a higher risk of marital breakdown. The work of Landis [18] brings this out very clearly, but the researches of other investigators [19] agree on the low incidence of breakdown when the couples share the same religious belief, particularly Roman Catholics, and a higher rate in mixed faith or in the total absence of religious adherence. Table 1 summarizes Landis' findings and those of two other major American studies.

Mixed Roman Catholic marriages have been the subject of much controversy as the Catholic Church imposes stringent conditions about the ceremony, which has to be carried out in

Table 1

Percentage of marriages of mixed and non-mixed religious faiths ending in divorce or separation, as revealed by studies of marriages in Michigan, Maryland and Washington

	Landis study, Michigan (Total 4,108)		Bell study, Maryland (Total 13,528)	Weeks study, Washington (Total 6,548)
	No.	%	%	%
Both Catholic	573	4·4	6·4	3·8
Both Jewish	96	5·2	4·6	
Both Protestant	2794	6·0	6·8	10·0
Mixed: Catholic Protestant	192	14·1	15·2	17·4
Both none	39	17·9	16·7	23·9
Protestant changed to Catholic	56	10·7		
Catholic changed to Protestant	57	10·6		
Protestant husband Catholic wife	90	6·7		
Catholic husband Protestant wife	102	20·6		
Husband none Wife Catholic	41	9·8		
Husband none Wife Protestant	84	19·0		

a Catholic Church, and the upbringing of the children, whom the non-Catholic party has to promise to bring up in the Catholic faith. It is claimed that these conditions, coupled with difficulties over birth control, are adequate reasons for the friction and marital disharmony. Indeed, the reasons seem to be so adequate that the controversy is left with both sides utterly convinced on the one hand of the iniquity of the Church's demands and on the other of the wisdom of maintaining the prohibition on mixed marriages, thus safeguarding the couple and their faith. On the surface there appears to be complete justification for whichever point of view is taken. This ignores the fact, however, that there are mixed Catholic marriages which are highly successful from every point of view. What is it that distinguishes one from the other? Heiss[20] asked a series of questions from a randomly chosen group of 1,167 people who lived in Manhattan, U.S.A., with the explicit purpose of elucidating the pre-marital characteristics of the religiously intermarried. 304 people had intermarried, including mixed marriages of Roman Catholics, Protestants, Jews and of no denomination, and 863 had married in the same faith.

He found that in general the mixed marriage couples had parents with marked secular leanings. Enquiring about the relationship between the subjects and their parents, he found that those who were dissatisfied in their early relationship with their parents are more likely to intermarry. Similarly, intermarriage was more likely among those who were in conflict with their parents, had tenuous ties with them or whose parental home exhibited strife. Now these are also exactly the home characteristics of those individuals who exhibit personality difficulties in adult life. There is here supportive evidence for the view that the single most important factor in marital instability is the personality of the partners and their relationship with their parents. In the absence of vulnerable traits, or strife and conflict in their own upbringing, the difficulties facing the partners of a mixed marriage are not exaggerated but successfully negotiated. When these personality difficulties do exist, religious differences over birth control and the religious upbringing of the children can become dangerous scapegoats for the failure to recognize and resolve the interpersonal struggle.

The last item in this chapter, *housing*, is included not because of the research it has attracted or the results obtained. In fact research workers have largely neglected the influence of housing on the quality of the marriage. Although there are few facts to guide, every worker in the field is acquainted with the innumerable couples, who, facing strained marital relations, lay the blame for this on poor housing and both plead and cajole for better accommodation. Frequently these are desperate and heart-rending pleas which cannot but evoke the deepest sympathy.

Inadequate accommodation for the needs of the family often means an exacerbation of noise and an increase of irritability as the various members impinge on one another. The presence of young children adds to the commotion and may have an adverse effect on the sexual life of the partners. Alternatively the discontent may be associated with excessive noise from next door or the neighbourhood and the neighbours may keep pets which are unwelcome, and have young children or adolescents whose behaviour leaves a great deal to be desired.

Such attempts as have been made to assess the housing factor have had to look for indirect evidence by measuring the frequency of quarrels and arguments between the various members of the family. One of the most thorough and up-to-date studies was carried out in Baltimore, U.S.A.[21] Here in a totally Negro population a thousand families were tested. One half of them were rehoused and the other half, who were on the waiting list, acted as controls. Both groups were tested before, and the test families after, the transfer. There was a small but not significant reduction in the incidence of quarrels and arguments between husband and wife in the group that were rehoused. Another study associated shortage of space with increased arguments and quarrels. These findings are thus so far indirect and incomplete. Further detailed clarification is needed.

FOUR

CHOOSING A PARTNER: INTELLIGENCE

EXAMINATION of the social factors associated with marital failure suggests that their adverse influence has to be interpreted with great caution.

In the United States census of 1950 a negative correlation was found between education and marital stability. A higher incidence of divorce was found among men with a low educational achievement. Since intelligence is one of the crucial factors in educational achievement, it could be argued through this indirect evidence that diminished intelligence is of importance in marital breakdown. Such a hypothesis would be highly attractive and would have widespread support in western societies where the intellect, or that faculty of mind by which man is able to control his environment, is regarded as his supreme endowment.

The figures of the census have to be interpreted with caution, however. While intelligence plays a major part in educational achievement, other factors such as the range and availability of educational facilities, motivation, emotional stability and other social pressures may all influence adversely the actual educational achievement of any individual. Despite these reservations, this hypothesis could be tested in its extreme form by examining marriage between partners certified as subnormal or mentally defective. One such study was carried out in England. It examined the records of 2,877 certified mental defectives. Two hundred and forty-two had married and of these 81 per cent were traced. The overall failure rate judged by divorce and permanent separation was 20 per cent. This is certainly higher than the highest national figure of 14 per cent but surprisingly the increase is not great and the authors comment: 'Nevertheless most of the marriages seemed to be reasonably happy and stable even when the families presented problems to others.' [22] Other studies have stressed this relatively successful outcome but also the need for the mentally defective mother to be emotionally stable and her resources not to be overtaxed by a family of a size beyond her capacity to cope. Indeed in the above study it was found that social adaptation was good in 64 per cent of the marriages with small families, dropping to 39 per cent among the larger families. Thus, given emotional stability and a mother who is not overtaxed, the results are surprisingly good. The limitations of intelligence, however, do undoubtedly influence the seeking and utilization of birth control and it is of paramount importance that such couples are assisted to achieve birth limitation in a reliable manner just as it is vital that they are helped to use fully the available social facilities in the community. Their limitations undoubtedly strain the resources of their neighbours and the social services but are not intrinsically destructive to the marriage.

According to our original hypothesis, namely that intelligence is the key to successful marriage, those with well above the average intelligence should hold the advantage with which society credits the intellectually gifted. The most careful analysis of such a group comes from the United States where the famous psychologist, Terman, one of the pioneers in marital research, followed up in an independent study the development of 1,500 intellectually superior children, starting in 1921.[23] By 1950–55 these children were adults in mid-life. 21 per cent of the men and 22 per cent of the women had a history of divorce, an incidence which approximates closely to that of the general population. This finding contradicts the belief that a high intelligence is in itself sufficient to prevent marital breakdown and confirms the very familiar clinical experience in which men and women of outstanding talents, carrying out important and complex jobs expertly, are nevertheless incapable of tackling their marital problems effectively. The dichotomy between intellect and emotions, intelligence and personality, much in evidence in a great deal of personality failure, is seen nowhere so acutely as in the presence of a totally unworkable marriage of two otherwise most successful and socially respected citizens.

FIVE

CHOOSING A PARTNER: PARENTAL IMAGE AND PERSONALITY NEEDS

PEOPLE of all ages have tried with variable success to ascertain the factors which bring a couple together. Physical beauty, intellectual prowess, social aptness and many other characteristics find regular favour. The actual choice often defies comprehension, remaining a mystery even to the couple themselves. A Swiss proverb describes marriage as a covered dish and another common saying suggests that marriages are made in heaven. These sayings point to the apparent blindness of the choice and the uncertainty of the outcome.

Modern research is slowly moving out of this complete uncertainty and sociologists have shown with considerable clarity that the place of residence, social class, race, age, intelligence, and religious affiliation define from the very start the field of eligible people within which the individual choice is made. Similarity in characteristics include more than these social features and Burgess and Wallin[24] who studied 1,000 engaged couples found similarities in a total of forty-seven characteristics covering religious affiliation and behaviour, family backgrounds, courtship behaviour, type of marriage (wife's work, number of children, sexual attitude), social participation (drinking and smoking habits, leisure time preferences, organizations attended), mutual friends and family relationships (attitude towards parents, brothers and sisters), and so on. This trend in similarity was also found in physical characteristics with a tendency for tall men to marry tall women and likewise for those of short stature.

While these social and physical characteristics delineate the field of eligible candidates, there still remains a wide choice from which the final selection is made. What other elements bring a particular man and woman together?

Freudian psychology, with its emphasis on the Oedipus complex, has greatly influenced the study of the parents' role.

The Oedipus complex is a key concept in the instinctual theory of personality development formulated by Freud. It describes the sexual attraction of the child to the parent of the opposite sex, with accompanying competitive hostile feelings towards the parent of the same sex. The complex is resolved with the gradual renunciation of these unconscious libidinal wishes, especially under the fear of castration as a punitive retaliation, with the concurrent drawing together of the boy with his father and the girl with her mother, technically called the process of identification – an identification therefore with the appropriate sex role. Based on this key Freudian hypothesis has been the assertion that men seek wives who resemble their mothers and women seek husbands who are like their fathers. Research has attempted to answer two questions here. First, whether, assertion apart, the general trend can be established that people tend to marry spouses who resemble the parent of the opposite sex and, if so, whether it is for the reasons maintained by Freudian psychology or for other reasons.

There is little doubt that some spouses are chosen with the image of the parent of the opposite sex in mind. Burgess and Wallin[25] give the following illustrations.

'Lucy's resemblance to my mother struck me. I think it was her walk and her smile. She had a lot of ambition. Both of them are ambitious. Mother has tried to make corrections in Dad. The young lady has the same tendency. They are not physically alike except that they walk the same way. They are the same height. My mother is rather lean, while Lucy is inclined to chubbiness. My mother is a dark blonde, and my fiancée is a brunette.'

'There is a physical resemblance between Carl and my father. My father now is heavy, but when he was young they were almost the same size. They might have been dead ringers for one another. They have blue eyes, sandy hair; undecided blond, I call it. They have long fingers. They are both very patient and unselfish. Neither one of them gets angry very suddenly or bears any grudges. They are both stubborn to a certain extent. They have minds of their own. They are reserved. They both have the same respect for women. Mother and I have often remarked about their resemblance. Others have too.'

But there are also examples where the spouse is chosen because he or she possesses the characteristics of the parent of the same sex.

'I would never want to marry anyone like my father, fond as I am of him. I couldn't stand being married to someone like him. I'm a little too much like him. My father came from a family which spoiled him and he had a very wonderful mother and was sort of tied to her apron strings. And Ed isn't. So that I don't have the competition with Ed's family that my mother is constantly faced with. Both Mother and Ed have open personalities – both are well liked and are good company. People will confide in Mother and also in Ed. I think they're very much alike in the way they look at people. Mother's much more easy in what she thinks of people than my father.'

A third example illustrates the desire to marry someone who is completely opposite to the parental figure.

'One thing I didn't like about my father was that he was too passive. I mean he agreed too much. My mother made all the plans, and although they worked out perfectly satisfactorily, I don't like that. I mean I don't like that for myself. One thing I always wanted was not to be the boss – I mean I always wanted someone who would stand up for his own rights. That was one thing wrong with those other boys. They were so 'in love' that everything I said was all right with them. And I wanted someone, I guess, who was a little stronger than that. At one time I thought Joey looked a little like a gangster. Other people don't think so, but you know what I mean. I think that's kind of significant now that I think of it. Because a gangster to me – well, a gangster has the connotation of being a real man. Wait – maybe it's because he hasn't got a weak-looking face – it has a certain strength – I think that comes closer to it.'

Finally a fourth and frequent pattern is a combination of those traits in the parents which were attractive to the child in the parent-child relationship.

'I'd say George was more like my father than my mother. Neither of them will let things slide – both are very punctual, very precise – that's probably because of their training. They both know what they want and they're out to get it. And I think they are both rather shrewd businessmen. Their personalities are very much the same. They're both great kidders and jokers. I'd say their personalities were very similar. But their temperaments are different – very different. George is like my father in personality and my mother in temperament. He's built very similar to my father. He's a little shorter, but he's heavy like my father. And they've both broad shoulders, large hands and feet. Mother has a very good disposition and shows it to everyone. She and George are two of the kindest people I've ever seen in my life. Neither would ever hurt anyone. George never forgets birthdays or Christmas or the little things. That's the primary attraction – because George is so very thoughtful and he seems to think more of me than most of the boys.'

These different points of view demonstrate the widely different choices made. Large-scale studies to examine the issue further are remarkably few. Strauss[26] was able to establish among 373 engaged or recently married persons a resemblance between the couple and parents which was greater than could be expected by chance or random choice. This was least marked in physical appearance and much more in evidence in the field of opinions, personality and temperament. These findings are in agreement with the view that parental images influence marital choice, but further examination of the data showed that the influential parent is not necessarily that of the opposite sex. Strauss believes that the important factor is, in fact, the presence of strongly positive affectional ties. Other investigators have tended towards this view; namely, that it is affectional bonds that knit together the parent and child.

The results of the research on the influence of the parental image are summarized by Burgess and Wallin.[27]

'One explanation appears applicable to the majority of cases. It is that the person tends to fall in love with someone who resembles the parent or parent surrogate with whom he was affectionately closest as a child. A secondary explanation seems to cover a much smaller proportion of cases. If there has been an unsatisfactory relation with one parent (typically of the other sex) the person is attracted to an individual with directly opposite characteristics.'

Another line of enquiry which has attracted a good deal of attention is the concept of personality needs. These needs can be few and simple, or multiple and very sophisticated. During the war Slater and Woodside[28] had the opportunity to investigate two hundred families of working- and lower-middle-class background. Some of their needs were simple in the extreme:

> 'I wanted a wife and was ready to marry anybody.'
> 'I thought I'd like a home of my own.'

The authors comment:

'One must remember the background – cramped living in an overcrowded parental home, but rarely the possibility of any privacy, often open parental discord and the constant struggle for economic independence. For the woman, the new home provides security, the escape from industry, from the supervision of the parents; for the man there are hopes of comfort, of something which will be his and will be built up by his own efforts.'

These needs for a home, independence, sexual fulfilment, and children are universal ones. A more personal note is struck in the brief comments of the husbands: '[She was] on the plain side, but I thought she was a dependable type. ...' '[She was] the type of person who doesn't want to dominate or make you do things. ...' And of a wife: 'He was so gentle and so kind, tolerant and patient, he had the best qualities for living together.'

The personal needs, which couples seek in marriage, are love and affection, confidence, sympathy, understanding, dependence, encouragement, intimate appreciation and emotional security.[29]

Such multiple reasons for marriage are given by a college girl in the United States:

'Laurence gives me what I want – he remembers birthdays. We have a lot in common, we like to do things together. ... It will be a sort of give-and-take relationship. Laurence doesn't tend to dominate me and tell me what to do and that satisfies me, I need that. And I can ask for advice and get it, but he doesn't insist on his way being the only way. We like to do pretty much the same things. We like sports that we can do together, and we like to dance. And I just like being together with him, which was something I could never do with any other boys ... There's a physical satisfaction too – we're compatible. He isn't too pressing that way – neither am I – so there is a nice balance. I like someone I can talk over things with, and sort of come back to, like discussing the day's work. I like someone I feel loves me too; I feel that very strongly. I don't want criticism but someone who understands my moods.'[30]

This particular example not only illustrates the pattern of expectation and fulfilment of mutual needs but it highlights its egalitarian characteristics. It is a reciprocal relationship based on understanding, in which authority, power, and decision-making are shared. It reflects the pronounced changes in woman's position achieved in the course of this century and the tendency for modern marriage to seek solutions in its day-to-day survival on the basis of a mutual interaction rather than in the playing out of rigidly conceived roles. There are obvious limits to this process, and some of the contemporary difficulties stem from the confusion and readjustment needed to meet these requirements.

Most studies have found that in meeting these personality needs the tendency for like to marry like as shown in the social and physical characteristics is matched in the similarity of personality traits.[31] *Assortative mating, however, has not only the possibility of bringing together stable personalities free from vulnerable traits but also the opposite.* Every major study associates marital disharmony and unhappiness with a high incidence of personality and neurotic difficulties in the partners.[32] A detailed analysis of these factors indicates that the absence of certain items enhances the chances of success and vice versa. The presence of marked fluctuations in mood, loneliness, undue sensitivity, feelings of guilt and remorse, lack of self-confidence, loss of temper, the need to dominate and inflexibility affect the marriage adversely. Summarizing their own and the findings of others, Burgess and Wallin[33] report that happily and unhappily married husbands and wives have the following contrasting characteristics:

Happily Married	*Unhappily Married*
Emotionally stable	Emotionally unstable
Considerate of others	Critical of others
Yielding	Dominating
Companionable	Isolated
Self-confident	Lack of self-confidence
Emotionally dependent	Emotionally self-sufficient

Some of these characteristics will be examined in detail in the following three chapters.

Up to the present the consensus of opinion has accepted the view that marital selection based on the principle of like marrying like means in practice that the personality and neurotic problems of one partner are matched by those of the other. This does undoubtedly take place but it does not exclude other possible mechanisms. It is possible for one partner to have started with a normal personality which has been so adversely affected in the course of the marriage by the spouse that by the time help is sought, both are equally disturbed. Evidence in support of this view has been brought forward from the spouses of psychiatrically ill patients by Kreitman.[34] Neurotic scores were measured in a psychiatric group of patients and their spouses and in a matched normal control group. With the passage of time neurotic scores increased in the spouses of the patients, particularly the wives, a finding not seen in the normal control group. More than one process may be operating but experience both in a marriage council and in psychiatric clinics provides ample evidence for the assortative mating hypothesis through the presence of marriages that break down in their earliest stages long before the mutual influencing has had a chance to operate. Clinical experience is further strengthened by the studies of Burgess and Wallin [24] who examined certain personality difficulties in their 1,000 engaged couples and later on in 666 of the same couples after some years of marriage. They conclude that marital unhappiness was influenced by adverse factors which remained constant and were present prior to marriage, and during the period of the engagement.

One authority has dissented from the unanimous conclusions of others regarding homogamy. For Winch,[35] the basis of attraction and selection has two phases. The social characteristics of age, social class, religion, and so on, determine the field of eligible candidates but the actual selection is determined by heterogamous motives. He puts forward the view that, with regard to the personality, people marry one another precisely because they see in each other characteristics which they lack and the other possesses *complementing* mutual needs. Thus those who fall in love are alike in their social traits but complementary in their psychological needs. For example, one who needs to be helped or nurtured is likely to be attracted by someone who needs to give help. Or someone who has a strong need for achievement will seek someone who has a corresponding need to abnegate. Clinical observations confirm that there is a great deal of truth in his theory.

It is very likely that both homogamous and heterogamous motives influence the ultimate choice. Whatever the mechanism, what makes marriage such a distinct entity is the fact that it brings about a close and intimate psychological relationship with marked affective components. The survival of every marriage depends on the capacity of the partners to meet the psychological needs which in turn requires a sufficient degree of maturity. Maturity is one of the commonest and most difficult words in the psychological repertory. What does emotional maturity imply?

There are various theories of personality development yet they all agree that emotional growth occurs by a series of phases. The child is expected to negotiate each phase successfully and to grapple with the challenge of the successive one.

The earliest phase is governed by marked dependency. It is a period of rudimentary behaviour largely influenced by needs of hunger, sleep and warmth. The next phase, covering the pre-school period, is characterized by increasing autonomy. This autonomy is achieved in movement, speech, bowel and bladder control. Concurrently increasing social contacts are made outside the home which are markedly extended later on at school. The range of initiative, social and intellectual, continues to increase rapidly until puberty. This biological upheaval brings into being adult sexual activity, adding this vital physical component to a sexual identity already established through patterning on mother and father. Adolescence leads to the final phase of separation between the young person and home, in which a job is found and heterosexual relationships established, ultimately leading to marriage.

Throughout these years the child is subjected to a series of emotional relationships between himself and the parents, the siblings, relatives and the social contacts outside the home. The vital relationship is that between himself and the parents from whom he receives security, affection, sexual identity, values, attitudes and social habits. In this intimate relationship the parents have the task of providing an umbrella of support which allows the maximum growth physically, intellectually and emotionally with the minimum danger to safety. Such a close and intimate relationship is needed for survival and growth. The growth-promoting relationship between child and parent is further extended at school. There, at home, and in the neighbourhood, siblings and their friends interact providing further opportunities for the cultivation and mastery of behaviour which involves initiative, industry and competition.

Marriage is a return to such a close and intimate union which allows the spouses to act as agents for further growth in their respective personalities as well as providing the requirements for procreation and the rearing of children. In order for the marital relationship to be viable it is necessary that both spouses have reached a sufficient degree of emotional independence, trust, self-acceptance, ability to receive and donate themselves to each other and an absence of excessive anxiety and aggression. These are essential characteristics for any close relationship without which marriage is not possible. Marital failure is intimately associated with the presence of one or both partners who have only partially or incompletely negotiated the various phases and the spouse is chosen as a means to *complete growth which should have been completed prior to marriage or to supply vital personal needs missing during the period of development.*

Psychological immaturity implies the presence of characteristics or needs which rightly belong to an earlier phase of development and it is these facets of the personality which are the major contributions to marital breakdown since the persons concerned are unable to meet the needs of the marital relationship. Thus the roots of marital failure must be considered to exist premaritally in the personality of the spouses. This does not mean that every such immature person is bound to have a marital breakdown. The capacity of the other partner to contain the difficulties will ultimately decide the outcome. When *two* immature persons marry through either homogamy or heterogamy the risk of failure is manifoldly increased.

The number of personality traits present in immaturity are many. In the following three chapters three of the commonest are presented and their influence in the early and later stages of the marriage examined. For the sake of clarity they are discussed singly and in isolation but more than one factor is frequently present in practice.

SIX

DEPENDENCY

ONE of the principal characteristics of human growth is the long period of childhood with its feature of dependence first on the mother and then on both parents. Life commences in a state of utter helplessness and survival depends on the ability of the parents to cater for the physical and emotional needs of the child, both being equally important. Emotional development is more complex and less obvious to a superficial examination. The infant and the child are responding to their environment continuously. This covers the pre-verbal period, the early phase of speech acquisition when communication is limited and the later phases when speech is fluent but the child lacks adequate control over its feelings. Throughout this early period the child feels its smallness, helplessness and insignificance and needs parents who will meet its anxieties, fears and terrors with trusty reassurance. It needs parents who will recognize its signals of distress and provide reliable and continuous comfort. Physical closeness and emotional reassurance are essential ingredients for emotional survival and growth just as food and shelter and systematic education are needed for physical and intellectual growth. Separation of child and parent, particularly in these early stages, is a threatening and traumatic experience unless the fears and apprehension thus generated are anticipated and handled adequately.

Human growth necessarily demands a gradual separation between child and parents, leading to the ultimate break when the young man and woman can leave home and feel confident about existing away from the emotional support of parents. *The failure to achieve a minimum of emotional independence is one of the main causes of marital breakdown.*

Two common family patterns contribute to emotional dependence. First is the presence of parents, one or both of whom are anxious people themselves, who may pass on this characteristic to their child. To such adverse inheritance is added the undoubted influence of the parental behaviour. Guarding against their own anxieties, they act in an over-protective manner ensuring that security or gratification are obtained only through the intervention of a continuous and protective watch exercised by them. The child learns to live with a world of anxiety experienced by his parents on his behalf and transmitted to him as the norm. If childhood illness has been in prominence, the ties between parent and child become closer and unsupported separation is fraught with even greater difficulties. Adolescence and the period of marriage is reached with little ability for detachment and independent existence, which is in fact dreaded either consciously or unconsciously. A separate self-existence now becomes a threat to personal survival and carries with it the most acute distress, which may express itself in a variety of physical and psychological manifestations of which anxiety and/or depression are frequent symptoms. The same result may be achieved, not only by over-protective parents but also by the presence of dominating, authoritarian ones who insist on making all the decisions and will not brook any independent action. The child may submit to this in the belief that this is for its own good or because rebellion carries the intolerable threat of being cut off from the source of love and emotional support without which existence appears extremely difficult, if not impossible.

Emotional dependence is often accompanied by a variable degree of anger and hostility. Independence, autonomy and self-control are the prized characteristics of emotional maturity. Their absence restricts, inhibits and places the sufferer in the hands of others for survival. Such a restriction of freedom is liable to be deeply resented and the parents gradually become objects of mixed feelings. They are needed for the support they afford and hated to the extent they symbolize personal limitations.

Marked emotional dependency may prohibit marriage altogether but, if the handicap is sufficiently overcome to allow marriage, it is still liable to endanger marital stability in a number of ways. Such unions may break up immediately or disintegrate slowly within the first year or two. Both partners may have marked traits of emotional dependency. Indeed, these very handicaps may have brought them together. Soon after the marriage, difficulties begin. If the couple live near their parents, there is the likelihood of frequent visits to the respective homes. These will become occasions of bitter resentment from the other partner who feels neglected or ignored. Whatever the merits of the individual complaints, both spouses are deeply divided within themselves, torn apart by the restless compulsion to return to the familiar, supportive and reliable background and the urge to move forward, to create a new life and meet the new needs of the partner. The parents have a vital part to play here. If they find the loss of their child difficult to tolerate and when they themselves need the support of the child as much as the latter needs them, they will do all they can to retrieve the loss. With little awareness or conscious desire to destroy the marriage, this is precisely what they will achieve by reinforcing their child's accusations and by destroying the good image of the spouse. When both parents are set to reclaim their children, the battle becomes totally unequal and the marriage has no chance of survival.

A marked feature of the emotionally dependent is their acute need for the physical presence of the partner who acts as a source of reassurance and reduces the *dread of aloneness*. If it is the wife who needs such support, she may find it pre-maritally at work, in her family or circle of friends. With the cessation of work immediately after marriage, particularly through a premarital pregnancy, there is not only the loss of companionship to cope with but also the growing anxiety about the coming child. In this instance the husband's presence is urgently needed and so is his reassurance.

Both these requirements may be excessively frightening to the husband similarly afflicted, who takes flight by working long hours of overtime, going out alone or with friends or bringing work home. An *impasse* is reached which may be resolved by the wife taking refuge with her parents, relatives or friends. In their absence, she may stay at home, waiting anxiously, sometimes despairingly. When the husband comes home he is attacked. The situation may be reversed with the wife absent at work or spending long visits with her parents and the husband, experiencing the same feelings, retaliates. Overt hostility leads to further mutual withdrawal and the vicious circle is set up for an early dissolution, rationalized on the familiar grounds of in-law interferences, neglect and cruelty.

An additional bitter disappointment may be the feeling of being let down or cheated by the partner who during courtship appeared attractively strong, reliable and reassuring. The dependent man may, for example, appear and act in exactly the opposite manner. This may be implicit in his job which carries outward manifestations of strength and courage such as being a member of the armed forces or the police, in behaviour which is expansive and grandiose, reassuringly knowledgeable and in attitudes which are fearless and forceful. Women, holding positions of reassuring authority, such as nurses or teachers, offer the promise of strength and security, and may act accordingly. These men and women are selected, consciously or unconsciously, in the hope and belief that they will continue their supportive role. When translated into the close and demanding relationship of marriage, they fail completely to measure up to the expectations of their spouses and their own emotional dependency is revealed in the intimacy of everyday living. They are now seen not only as inadequate but also as unreliable and deceitful people who have trapped their partners.

These early disappointments are further aggravated by the arrival of a baby which increases the wife's need of support. This in turn aggravates the husband's anxiety through his inability to meet the new demands and further threatens his own precarious hold over his wife. The advocacy of a baby to 'cement' such a marriage may well prove to be the death knell for such a union.

Such marriages may come to an abrupt end, or they may stagger on for a while with repeated episodes of separation and return to their families, reuniting for short periods, leading finally to either a dissolution or to a gradual resolution of the conflict. The early dissolution of a marriage may be brought about by another less frequent pattern in which the couple come together on the basis of a mutual inability to accept anyone else except another rebel. Marked antagonism towards parents, or those in authority, coupled with an intense desire to escape from them, brings about these unions in which the main motive is, consciously or unconsciously, to be freed from and punish those who have held sway over their lives until then. After the initial gusto of rejoicing in the defeat of the elders, the energies and motivations which united the couple prior to marriage are now directed towards one another. Marriage becomes a dangerous trap where all their old fears of being subjected to and dominated by another are resuscitated. This stress leads to withdrawal and further expressions of independence. Reconciliation is only possible along lines which enable mutual acceptance of each other without the danger of feeling dominated. If this is not possible the marriage inevitably breaks up.

The various patterns described so far are conspicuous by the absence of any qualities of complementarity. In most marriages there is a sharing of tasks and performances in which the spouses act according to their particular talents, offering to each other the fruit of their own special abilities. Broadly speaking, the husband will be responsible for the executive, practical and financial aspects of the marriage while the wife, apart from child-bearing, has traditionally been looked upon as the mainstay for the affectionate, nurturing, emotional needs of the family with specific responsibility for managing the home. These are extremely broad generalizations which are being modified to a considerable degree, particularly through the changing role of women. The point remains that, however fluid, the roles undertaken are different and contribute to the complementary needs of the spouses in such a way that neither feels unduly subordinated or dominated by the other. A relationship of equality is achieved through different contributions of equivalent significance.

There are marriages, however, which initially can only exist on the basis of a domination-submission relationship. The person with strong dependent needs seeks a partner who will provide a continuity of parental support. The spouse will be cast in this role, treated with similar expectations, and the same mixed feelings of love and hate. The dominant partner may be the husband or the wife. He or she will continue in the parental role of taking the vital decisions, protecting the spouse from worry by taking on the burdens of everyday life.

The dependent personality may invest the dominant supporting partner with all the qualities of the key parental figure whose place they have taken. In the original child-parent relationship the hostility may have been unconscious. If conscious, it was difficult to express because of the guilt aroused and the anxiety of losing the affection of the most important being in the world. In marriage the same mixed feelings exist. Gradually, however, the fear may diminish and, little by little, increased hostility emerges with recurrent criticism and sniping. If the husband is the submissive partner, he will criticize his wife's capacity as housewife and mother. While accepting her decisions and arrangements, he will rejoice at her discomfort and blame her excessively for anything that goes wrong. He will allow her to control and discipline the children but will take their side against her whenever he can. When the wife finds herself in this role she will criticize his manly failures, particularly if he does not obtain promotion at work. The wife possesses ultimately the strongest deterrent, her ability to withhold sexual intercourse, a weapon which may be used extensively as a means of revenging herself.

Both will use the presence of relatives and friends as auxiliary resources to launch an attack which they would otherwise be afraid to carry out alone. At times the frustration and anger of the weaker partner will reach breaking point, when all control is lost and physical violence inflicted. Alcohol aids and abets this situation allowing pent up feelings of rage to be discharged in an uninhibited manner. Thousands of divorces obtained on the grounds of cruelty arise in an escalation of hostility following many years of bickering and quarrelling of this nature.

With the passage of time two other distinct developments occur. Most commonly the dependent spouse may mature slowly to a point where, after many years of apparent harmony, the original relationship is no longer a satisfactory basis for marriage. *Emotional growth and the changes that occur with it provide a major source of disharmony leading to the breakdown of marriage.*

This maturation is the end result of a variety of processes. Success at work, with promotion, leads to greater responsibility and, in turn, greater realization of what the person is capable of achieving. This brings about a great deal of reassurance. Hitherto frightening situations, such as facing opposition, anger from others and the possibility of rejection, were avoided at any price by compromise and submission or by placation. As these fears recede, opposition, disapproval, anger and even rejection are survived without dread and the terror of personal extinction. Every painful encounter successfully negotiated becomes the springboard for further emotional and social challenges. Success generates success but, even more important, convinces the person that personal survival can withstand the occasional rejection, defeat, temporary isolation and criticism from others. These are some of the means by which all emotional growth takes place but its impact and consequences on those who have started their independent existence in a hesitant manner, needing the equivalent of a parental figure to keep an eye on them, is naturally much greater.

If it is the husband who is changing, having asserted himself in his work situation, he will wish to do likewise at home. Decisions taken for years by the wife will no longer receive rubber-stamp approval. If the wife fails to recognize the change, she will block his attempts either by refusing to accept his interventions or by insisting on improving and changing all his contributions. She will have an answer and a better one to everything he suggests. After all, she has been doing this for years and does not see the need for change after all this period. If his early attempts do not match initially her expertise, this will be ruthlessly exposed. As far as the children are concerned, he may wish to contribute to their upbringing. This will threaten the bonds created by the mother with her children and will be resented passively or actively by pointing out to the children his previous failure to be concerned with them.

Attempts on his part to live an independent life outside the home will be bitterly resented. She will accuse him of ignoring their original friends (usually hers) on the grounds that they are not good enough for him and that he is getting above his station. Finally, any signs of sexual initiative or changed requirements in affection will be spurned and he will be reproached for his sexual greed and irresponsibility.

One or more of these responses will be interpreted by the husband as an attempt to reduce him to his customary unimportant subordinate and relatively impotent role, creating deep resentment in him. He will begin to see his wife more as a jailer than a spouse. He will gradually discover that, with all his new needs blocked, he will have nothing in common with her. He will, in fact, have outgrown the necessity for her presence and, without any apparent outward change in his life, he will find himself separated by a gulf from her. It will be described as falling out of love. Being in love implies a meaningful relationship in which needs are met and the potential for growth acknowledged and encouraged. He is not acknowledged, recognized or accepted in his new capacity and, with this rejection, he no longer finds the relationship meaningful.

His needs blocked at home, there is always someone in the office, factory or next door who is prepared to treat him as worthwhile and precious and imperceptibly, without realizing it, he will find himself out of love with his wife and in love with someone else. When his adultery is discovered or self-disclosed, this will provoke the enraged fury of his wife, who will feel she has been treated irresponsibly and unfairly. Relatives, friends and acquaintances will side with her and so will the law as it stands at present, for technically he has committed *the* matrimonial offence. He will be the guilty party and no one, probably not even he himself, will realize that only now has he reached the moment of sufficient emotional independence to make a free choice. He can now relate to someone who is not a parental figure but an adult person with whom he can share his life on the basis of equality and complementarity.

But the price is heavy. Children exist with whom there are bonds of affection. The decision to part is an agonizing one.

His wife has her own needs and, however strong his case may be, she has claims on his loyalty and original vows. Guilt feelings abound. Paradoxically sometimes it is at this point that the dominant spouse breaks down and exposes her or his own dependency which has been camouflaged up to that point with an apparently strong personality. The presence of this reality may allow the necessary adjustments to render the marriage viable on a different basis. Unfortunately for the majority who reach the divorce courts there is no last-minute change of heart.

If the wife is the dependent personality her own emotional maturation will correspond closely to the development described for the husband and a similar course will follow.

What are the reasons for the failure of adaptation on the part of the dominant partner? They may not be aware of, or understand, the changes that are taking place in their spouses. Marital counselling can and does assist considerably in such a situation by pointing out the nature of the change in the relationship. Even with this assistance, however, adaptation may be difficult. The behavioural pattern may be deeply ingrained. More serious is the situation where the dominant partner does not wish to change. This resistance is frequently associated with a childhood background in which the dominant spouse has been himself the subject of domination. Unable to assert themselves in their home, they choose a dependent partner through whom unfulfilled needs of assertion are met. They can control their partner and they feel safe only in this situation. The daughter, for example, seeing her mother and herself treated indifferently and harshly by her father will ensure this does not happen to her. She chooses a husband who is dependent on her. In this way she feels safe and initially his needs are met, particularly if, as is usual, he comes from a house where his own mother dominated the household. When the time comes to assert himself, the wife feels acutely threatened as the anxieties about her mother's treatment are revived. Here flexibility is at its minimum and counselling can assist by helping her to see what is the nature of her reluctance to face the reality of the situation.

An alternative situation arises in which maturation of the dependent partner does not occur and the original pattern continues in the fifth and sixth decade. If the needs of the dominant partner remain unchanged then no difficulty arises. But change is also possible for the dominant partner. The position is reached in which the husband and the wife, after providing many years of support, begin to need urgently a change in the partner. If the wife has been the nurturing partner, there may be a sudden transformation in her fifth decade. This is the decade with a powerful impact on her, a reminder of her passing years and the urgency to be fulfilled as a woman. The acceptance of the inadequacies in her husband suddenly becomes intolerable. He is pushed frantically to perform in a manly manner sexually and to take on the role of head of the household. Decisions about the house, the children and the future are placed in his lap and an outrageous onslaught is unleashed if he does not rise to the occasion. If the husband has been developing in his own right, he can respond to the new demands. If he has not, the urgency and magnitude of her requirements will precipitate a crisis beyond his comprehension. The demands for greater sexual activity may well precipitate complete impotence. The pressure to take on hitherto unrecognized responsibilities will produce a wave of anxiety and ineffectual activity.

Further frustrated by this response, the wife will pour out a stream of criticism and abuse mingled with hostile taunting. Increasing frustration with an unresolved marital situation may well drive her into an extra-marital affair in which she seeks recognition and sexual satisfaction. If, in the process, she becomes pregnant, her predicament, already difficult, may become intolerable, producing a characteristic situation in which abortion is sought as a desperate measure.

If the affair is discovered, even without a pregnancy, her behaviour will bring down on her head the social and moral disapproval of relatives and friends who may find the whole incident incomprehensible and inexplicable. Indeed, the woman herself, if pressed for explanation, may not fully understand the motivating pressures within herself. In her predicament it is only too easy for onlookers to condemn her apparent pleasure-seeking excursions. She herself will be torn between her overwhelming desire to seek fulfilment before she feels it is too late and the agonizing choice of abandoning her children and their father. Once again, only a penetrating awareness of the reality of the situation will allow a detached appraisal, in which condemnation follows only at the last, if at all. Instead, an attempt is made, through marriage counselling, to mobilize in the husband any latent capacities.

The same course of events applies when the husband is the dominant partner. Here the deficiencies of the wife, tolerated until now, become the focal point of the unexpected attack. Her personal appearance, and her ability to run the home and look after the children all become suddenly objects of bitter complaint. Sexual dissatisfaction is seized upon particularly if accentuated by menopausal changes. As with the wife, the existing emotional aridity is no longer tolerable. The temptation to seek the solution in an extra-marital affair or with a new partner is very strong and, as with the wife, demonstrates that the motives behind adultery are usually much more complex than simple pleasure-seeking. Thus dependency may destroy a marriage right at the very beginning or after many years of marriage during which changes have occurred unilaterally and are not matched in the partner.

SEVEN

DEPRIVATION

IN the last chapter the significance of emotional dependence was considered. The acquisition of independence is one of the essential processes that takes place within the family allowing the gradual separation between child and parent so that the emerging person can experience and accept themselves as separate and capable of surviving without the support of parents or parent surrogate. In addition to emotional independence the growing person needs to experience approval, affection and tender physical closeness.

Approval is gained by the growing awareness that one is treated as a subject worthy of acknowledgement and acceptance, feeling wanted, trusted and appreciated for one's own sake. Affection is experienced through this approval and by means of affectionate expressions such as smiles, kisses and acts of tenderness which are appropriate to the particular culture. Finally, there is need for physical closeness first experienced in the arms of the mother and then through the father. Approval, affection and physical closeness are as much a necessity for normal human growth as is food, and their absolute or relative absence leads to deprivation and insecurity, the second damaging agent to a marital relationship.

The deprivation may be overt and complete. The illegitimate abandoned child, the illegitimate child with only one parent, or the child who has lost one or both parents by death or desertion without adequate substitutes are common examples.

The deprivation may be subtly hidden but equally complete as with parents who are present but completely preoccupied with themselves or their jobs and who hand over the upbringing of their children to relatives, nannies or boarding schools. Here the child may be aware of parental withdrawal and feel deeply hurt, or being aware of their indifference and, finding this extremely painful, he may idealize the parents, particularly if they have special attributes of beauty, talents or skills. Thus the child enters into a distant relationship which idealizes but cannot get close, with complete unawareness of the underlying frustration and anger. All these feelings can be repeated in the marital situation when an idealized parent substitute is chosen as the spouse.

The deprivation may be overt but partial and this may take a number of forms. The parent may find emotional closeness extremely difficult but may be capable and willing to relate intellectually or through physical skills with the child. The statement 'I admired my father (or mother) because they were hard-working, talented, upright, honest, and so on, but I could not get close to them' or 'they had no time for me' are frequent utterances in the personal history of the spouses.

Finally, there is deprivation which is covert and partial. This usually means an intact home situation where both parents are present but not available due to their own psychological or physical limitations. Parents, who are perpetual worriers or frequently ill, partially or permanently incapacitated render themselves unavailable through circumstances beyond their control. Similarly in a very large family there may not be enough time or attention to go round and some of the children may suffer as a consequence.

In all these situations the parental contribution which effects deprivation has been emphasized. This may not always be the case. The child's constitution may make acceptance of affection difficult or its need may be in excess of what is available. Some children find physical closeness intolerable and can only tolerate a minimum degree of embracing or cuddling. Others need physical contact which appears excessive. Such traits may prevent the child from experiencing affection or in turn render it very difficult to return it.

Thus parental attitudes or the child's disposition or a combination of both contribute to a variable degree to emotional deprivation. The stability of the marriage will depend on the intensity of this feeling and on the capacity of the partners to adjust to these traits in each other. Just as with emotional dependency, deprivation can make its impact immediately in the marriage or influence it after some years.

Marriages breaking down in the first two to three years may do so as a result of emotional dependence or the union of two extremely deprived individuals. The couple making up such a marriage consist usually of shy, diffident people who find their insufficiencies, loneliness and isolation a common bond. Both are seeking those very qualities of security, affection and stability of which they have an inordinate need and a total incapacity to reciprocate. They start their relationship with enormous expectations of mutual fulfilment. Shortly after the marriage their hopes begin to fade and there begins a bitter exchange of mutual recriminations and quarrels. The multitude of insufficiencies and inadequacies, real or phantasized, are skilfully selected and presented to one another accompanied by all the frustration and anger from feeling let down and unfulfilled. The disappointment is acute as the hopes raised beforehand were unrealistically high. Their own shortcomings and exaggerated demands are ignored or underrated.

Let us take, for example, the marriage of Mr and Mrs S. Looking at such a marriage from the outside it is hard to show that their demands are excessive, such is their intense need for affection, support and reassurance. They sought help from a marriage council. They were seen separately and gave a bitter and hostile account of each other. They were both only children. She was Irish and a schoolteacher. Her mother had been kind and affectionate but a marked worrier who spent a good deal of her time in bed with real and imaginary complaints. Her father was a farmer, distant and preoccupied with his work. Her childhood was solitary and most of her energy was directed towards educational matters. Her periods came when she was fourteen, a frightening experience, which was not helped by her mother's curt dismissal of the event with some practical advice about sanitary towels. At university she had no boy-friends and her only social outlet was choir singing. She started teaching in a primary school in England and met her husband in the choir of their local church. His background was similar. He was the only son of an anxious mother and a shy, withdrawn father, who concentrated on his gardening and his civil service job. Friends were not welcomed in the house and he had few contacts as he grew up. He indulged excessively in masturbation, his solitary comfort and a source of much guilt and fear. His wife was his first and only girl-friend. They met at a party organized for the choir. They noticed each other sitting at the opposite ends of the hall on their own and uninvolved with the others. He approached her and they struck up a friendship which led to marriage after a year. Marriage was a disappointment to both of them. She did not care for sexual intercourse and submitted to it reluctantly. After the birth of her child she could not tolerate it at all.

'He only thinks of sex. . . . I can't stand him. He is mean with money. . . . I never know how much he earns. He makes an allowance to me which is just not enough and when I complain, he says it is my incompetence. He never takes me out, he just sits at home and reads or watches the television. Later on in bed he expects me to be all coy and interested. I think he is just selfish. All he wants is my body and even when we did make love it was all over before I knew it had started. He simply doesn't care about me.'

He in turn complained of her frigidity. 'It was always an ordeal for her! He denied frequent demands. 'We went for weeks without it, even before the baby came. After my little girl was born, I did not count any more. I suppose we both need more attention than we are capable of giving to one another. I want to try if only she would give me a chance.' Her reply was 'He only says that because he wants sex; all that I've got left now is my girl.'

This couple exemplify the recurrent complaints in this situation. Money, time, material goods, suitable accommodation (though not in this case) are the overt complaints which, independent of their own significance, signify the underlying need to feel wanted, appreciated and reassured. When the needs are primarily emotional and severe, material inadequacies provide a suitable vehicle to express the underlying frustration. When genuine material deprivation is present, this often blurs the real issue which remains and explains the failure to improve relations even after conditions have improved.

Sexual relations have a vital part in such a relationship. The deprivation experienced by the husband is concentrated on sexual matters. Sexual intercourse carries a promise of repeated and easily available fulfilment. The need is so urgent that little care is given to the affectional needs of the wife and such indifference is unfortunately often coupled with a quick male orgasm which leaves the wife dissatisfied. Such an experience, frequently repeated in the early months of marriage, reminds the deprived wife of a similar earlier situation in which she felt abandoned and unloved. The word 'used' is the one most frequently uttered by wives of all social classes in these circumstances. It is a word which fully conveys the experience of continuous deprivation in which the husband appears to get a great deal of satisfaction while the wife is left utterly and completely unmoved or, even worse, partially aroused, tense and frustrated at the end of the act. The husband is gradually experienced as an exploiter.

He is usually completely unaware of these feelings until the advent of pregnancy. Pregnancy may be used, deliberately or unconsciously, by the wife to reduce or suspend sexual relations and the denial is continued after the birth of the child. Her denial sets up a mounting frustration since sexual intercourse had acted as an unrecognized source of therapy up till then. Its cessation resuscitates the gnawing and painful feelings of deprivation. These feelings are further aggravated by the preoccupation of the mother with the new-born child, which isolates her still more from the husband. The absence of intercourse and the lack of attention, both of which can be explained away by the wife, create a desperate situation. The need for reassurance elsewhere mounts and may lead to the use of prostitutes, extra-marital affairs and may finally lead to desertion. Such behaviour appears and is interpreted by the wife as callous and cruel. Indeed it would be so if the offending husband had an alternative. Insatiable craving must be alleviated at any price.

Such marriages may end under the present law on a variety of grounds, such as cruelty, adultery and/or desertion. Here as elsewhere it is perfectly clear that adultery and/or cruelty are the outcome of an existing situation rather than contributing to it. Reconciliation is possible when the needs of both spouses are taken into account and they are helped to achieve this, at least in part. The practical difficulty, and it is a very real one, is to convince the partners that they are capable of fulfilling one another if their demands are modified and their behaviour becomes less destructive. Opposing such a reconciliation is the ever present phantasy that somewhere there exists someone who will meet all their needs and this magical hope can defeat all efforts of reconciliation.

The need for security and affection may be considerable and yet prove neither overwhelming nor completely unanswered by the partner. This is the situation in which the marriage continues for a number of years, depending for its survival on a number of factors precariously balanced. The first of these is the presence of one spouse whose needs are neither as great nor as acute as those of the partner. In such a relationship the more mature person can accept and tolerate the attention-seeking or 'showing off' behaviour of their partner. Attention-seeking is particularly in evidence at parties when the spouse is ignored and attention is monopolized with or without marked flirtation. Attention-seeking may, of course, go beyond this and involve repeated extra-marital affairs with or without the knowledge of the partner. Such behaviour may be tolerated for years in the hope that the frequent explanations, apologies and solemn promises for a change will be observed. After ten, fifteen or twenty years, especially when children have grown up, the tolerant spouse, usually the wife, gives up and terminates the contract. At some stage hope is abandoned and the doubt becomes a certainty that the husband or wife is unlikely to change or 'grow up'.

Another common situation is the presence of two moderately deprived persons who derive sufficient complementary satisfaction to preserve the union but need more. The extra may be sought in a competitive fashion so that the presence of others becomes the battleground for their attention. To a detached observer this looks like the squabbling of siblings for parental attention and indeed the behaviour may be very similar. The spouses contradict, criticize and appear anxious to defeat one another in order that notice may be taken of them. If the husband wins the particular round, the wife's frustration and anger may be repaid in bed by withdrawal of sexual favours and anger may be expressed by either defeated party through withdrawal, sulking or provocative behaviour. Despite repeated outbursts a *modus vivendi* may be reached unless the provocation becomes excessive for one of the partners.

Arising from this very situation, of two moderately deprived persons remaining together but finding each other partially insufficient, is the *ménage à trois* solution. The insufficiency of the partner may be experienced sexually, intellectually, socially or in other characteristics. A second person is selected to meet the missing requirements, creating a triangular or even a quadrangular situation in which the husband relates to his legal wife but has a semi-permanent relationship with another woman and vice versa for the wife. This is much more than an extra-marital affair of a limited duration or even a series of extra-marital affairs since the 'spouse' remains in a continuous relationship for a number of years. The presence of the extra person may be unknown to the partner but occasionally it is not only known but actively encouraged. The quadrangular situation where both the husband and the wife are having an affair with the approval of the other is the epitome of this.

The need to bring a third person into the marriage may be the outcome of a subtle change in the marital relationship, as is shown in the following example.

An attractive, vivacious woman of thirty-two was advised to seek psychological help for her excessive barbiturate intake. Her marital history disclosed that she had been married for nine years, had no children, was apparently contented with her husband but could not break a very active relationship with a man who was her husband's best friend. The relationship was well known to her husband, who at the interview confirmed the harmony of their sexual life, had no complaints against his wife, and would have loved the affair to end but could not take the initiative to do so. Despite his frustration and anger he was not prepared to risk a break with his wife and so condoned her behaviour and the frequent visits to his friend's house where he knew intercourse took place, with only the merest grumble.

The husband was extremely busy in a job which kept him away from home for long hours. His wife had grown up in a home where her mother was a teacher who had worked most of her childhood to support the family due to the husband's chronic incapacity. She needed a great deal of affection and during several interviews openly expressed her complete satisfaction with her husband, when he was available. She needed constant reassurance and her frustration mounted rapidly if left alone, at which point she rang her boy-friend. When her husband was busy in the office she would go to her friend's flat from which her husband would collect her later in the evening. She was well aware of the inconsistency of her position and terrified that her husband would one day cease his toleration but neither of these anxieties was sufficient to quench her need for attention.

Such a triangular situation can be resolved. This can be achieved either through the gradual diminution of need in the deprived partner or the increased availability of the spouse. If neither of these conditions is met, then the marriage may ultimately break down at a point where the aggrieved spouse feels strong enough to challenge or reject the arrangement.

Finally, there is the situation in which the deprived spouse resorts neither to extra-marital relationships nor to a semi-permanent triangular situation. Efforts persist for a long time to obtain from the spouse what is needed, all without avail and with minimal and unreliable spurts of support. This may be tolerated for a long time for the sake of the children or for religious and other motives, until a situation is reached where years of aridity create an intolerable situation and the husband or wife simply decide to go, even twenty years after marriage.

Mr and Mrs B. had reached this point after twenty-two years of marriage. He was forty-seven, she forty-two. He was a consultant in the health service with a busy private practice. She had qualified as a doctor but had not been allowed to proceed with a professional career. The husband had not considered it appropriate that his wife should work. She raised a family of two children who were now in university. A close examination of their marital relationship revealed the absence of sexual relationship for some ten years through the husband's impotence. They spent hardly any time together, excused on the grounds of his professional work and amply rationalized by his ability to maintain a very expensive way of life in which his wife and children lacked nothing materially.

'It is true that he is most generous with money but I hardly see him except on holiday, and even then he interrupted it last year for an urgent consultation. He can't show any emotion and when we did have intercourse, which was a long time ago, I got nothing from it. I have come to realize in the last few months that I have lived with an efficient machine and I have been starved of all the things I long for.'

At the time of the interview she was having a deeply satisfying relationship with a businessman and she was determined to leave her husband.

Marital reconciliation ultimately depends on the ability of the spouses to change sufficiently to meet each other's minimal needs. This can only be done when change is possible and marriage counselling has to accept the reality of a situation in which one or both partners are totally incapable of meeting each other's legitimate needs, as in the above couple. The marriage may not end with a divorce and remarriage. Partners may simply separate with or without a new relationship depending on their religious and social beliefs and their willingness to risk any further disappointments.

EIGHT

SELF-ESTEEM

'I AM surrounded by a husband who adores me, two lovely affectionate children and yet I can enjoy neither because I don't feel I deserve it.'

Complete or partial rejection of self as inferior, bad, and unworthy of love completes the triad of the significant traits in personality which contribute to marital breakdown. The above wife's cry can be heard repeatedly in personal accounts of marital strife.

In the course of development the child will form a separate identity, which will depend partially on its own inner experience of itself and partially on its experience of itself in the hands of others, particularly the parents. From its earliest years it will begin to associate parental approval with feeling good; disapproval and punishment with feelings of guilt and badness. Badness and goodness become essential guiding experiences, later to be reinforced by religion and society. Good feelings are associated with closeness to the loved one, badness with rejection and alienation.

The development of these feelings depends on the make up of the child and its capacity to attract approval and the ability of the parents to communicate to their child the certainty of its being lovable and good. In the last chapter, deprivation was dealt with as an experience in which the growing person was denied some of the essential ingredients for human growth, approval, protection, affection, love and tenderness, creating a yearning need which is relentlessly sought after later on in life. Such a deprivation leaves not only a gap in the actual needs of the person but is frequently associated with a sense of unworthiness. During the earliest years when the young child experiences deprivation, absolute or partial, it is not in a position to reason out the appropriate explanation for the absence of comfort and satisfaction. If first mother and then father are unavailable, available in a limited way or if the child's needs are disapproved of, it begins to feel *bad for needing*. This is the period when it begins to experience badness unconditionally. Since its needs are inevitable, how these are met will give it a sense of being good or bad. If bad feelings are predominantly experienced, the child frequently absolves the parents from responsibility. The goodness of the parents must be preserved at any price. Thus badness, guilt and disapproval become deeply ingrained experiences which are felt to belong entirely to oneself.

The parents can and frequently do play a major role in inculcating such negative feelings in the way they handle the child through its various phases. The earliest need is for food and the capacity to endure the frustration of hunger is minimal. Attempts to organize a feeding schedule which suits the mother will leave the child frustrated. Crying may indicate this, but in the pre-verbal stage it may also indicate pain, discomfort, fear of aloneness, all equally terrifying experiences which require urgent attention. At this age a good deal of the self is experienced through these elementary needs. Meeting them effectively will lay the foundations of self-acceptance without conflict.

The next phase is concerned with bowel and bladder control and will coincide with a marked phase of increasing autonomy. The child will soon begin to distinguish behaviour that proves acceptable, making it feel good, from that which is unacceptable, bad and punishable. If the parents recognize the frustration and temper tantrums of this stage as a necessary part of autonomy to be negotiated with patience rather than scorn or punishment, 'good' feelings will predominate. In addition, a great deal of disapproval and guilt may be engendered if the speed with which bowel and bladder control is desired exceeds the child's capacity. The child needs to emerge from the preschool phase knowing that it can have needs and experiences of autonomy without feeling bad or guilty about them, with abundant access to both parents, who, through their physical and emotional contact, give it a sense of being welcomed and wanted unconditionally.

Unwanted pregnancies, the presence of a child of the opposite sex to that desired, backwardness, awkwardness, all lead to a variable degree of rejection which is immediately sensed by the child. This is particularly the case when a pregnancy out of wedlock compels a couple to marry. If the marriage is not successful, the child is a convenient scapegoat and is made to carry a heavy burden of responsibility for the marital breakdown.

Rejection can also be engendered by the child's characteristics which are similar to those possessed and rejected by the parents in themselves. The child now becomes the victim of the parents' own unresolved feelings of inadequacy and badness. This is particularly in evidence during the school period when the child fails to live up to the expectations of the parents. These may be well beyond its capacities, leaving it with an increasing awareness of being incapable of pleasing the most important persons in the world. This growing certainty of being unable to please, which may extend in other spheres of activity, continues later on and is repeated in the marital relationship. The parents may, in fact, be working through the child their own unfulfilled ambitions, success being vital for their own requirements. The child acquires a sense of badness through its inability to acquit itself satisfactorily in their eyes. This difficulty takes a particular form in a family where all but one of the children manage to please the parents or, alternatively, only one achieves the ambitions of the parent, the rest being relegated to comparative insignificance.

All this involves the behaviour of the parents who in the early years carry a special responsibility not to endow the child with a sense of unconditional badness. Needs have to be met, socialization effected, values inculcated without depriving the child of the sense of feeling good, worthy of love, and acceptable to others. Nevertheless, feelings of badness are not entirely the responsibility of parents.

Much of the work of the dynamic schools of psychology is concerned with the child's inner experience of itself particularly with regard to its feelings of aggression. Freud postulated two basic instincts, sexual and aggressive as the foundations on which the personality develops. Few will accept such a limited concept today but no one will deny the importance of aggression. Melanie Klein traced aggressive feelings back to their earliest phase when the baby is sucking at the breast. The breast is experienced as an object standing for the whole mother. On some occasions it is experienced as a 'good' breast which is satisfying and fulfilling, at other times as a 'bad' one when frustrating and unyielding. These experiences are first internalized, the child feeling alternatively good and bad feelings and then externalized through projection. Thus the child's immediate world is populated with good and bad objects from which it expects love and anger.

All goes well when the feelings experienced are predominantly good which are projected and re-experienced as such. When the feelings are bad, they are similarly projected but the surrounding world is now experienced as threatening, punishing and persecutory. These experiences may be based on reality, as we have just seen by the presence of a threatening and punishing mother but such feelings may also be based on the child's own phantasies (which can, of course, be reinforced by reality). Melanie Klein sought to understand further such bad feelings by investigating the origins of envy and greed. The breast, standing for the whole mother, appears to the child to possess everything good and valuable compared with its own emptiness. Envy seeks to destroy this superiority of the mother and is contrasted with greed which seeks to possess the breast entirely, to appropriate it for itself. Destruction or incorporation leave the child with horrifying fears of damaging, injuring and losing the good mother.

This instinctual theory of personality-development is but one of many alternative explanations for the origin of bad feelings. The young child is a mass of seething needs, physical and emotional. Frustration is an early and repeated experience even when it is handled by the most understanding and benevolent parents. Frustration is frequently accompanied by anger and punishment. Thus parents, who one moment are the source of love and fulfilment are, on another occasion, the agents of disapproval, retaliation and punishment. The child has to adapt to this reality, to conform and use all available techniques for limiting disapproval. It can do this in several ways.

Withdrawal from a frustrating situation with the suppression of anger, and abandonment of gratification thus ensuring continuing parental acceptance is one possibility. This may become an established pattern in the personality carried over into marriage in which either spouse rapidly withdraws when they cannot easily experience gratification, their anger aroused but repressed. This is a complicated situation, for just as in childhood, the spouses badly want gratification. Failing to obtain it, they withdraw resentfully, unfulfilled, angry and without the means of redress. Another solution has already been mentioned. The child at this early stage cannot blame mother or father if things go wrong. It must be its own fault and it becomes saddled with its own badness. The parent must be experienced as a good person and the way of doing this is to idealize them. They are good in every possible way, while the child by comparison is bad in every way. This idealization may or may not be accompanied by repressed anger but it can certainly be carried over into marriage. The spouse is now selected unconsciously on the basis of the idealized parent. He or she is good and by comparison the spouse is bad and feels that whatever goes wrong is their fault. A third possibility is to regress. If growing up means a denial of previously permissible gratification then it is not worth while. Retiring to an earlier emotional phase is a recurrent experience noticed in children under stress and this behaviour is also repeated in adulthood. Regression is frequently accomplished through ill health which is always real in the sense that the person is experiencing the symptoms even though the basis is emotionally conditioned.

Feelings of badness are intimately associated with feelings of inadequacy and inferiority. It was Adler who stressed the importance of physical, intellectual and social deficits leading to feelings of inferiority and the need to compensate through power.

An acceptance of self as a person capable of love and worthy to receive it, free from exaggerated feelings of inadequacy, or destructiveness and hostility are the essential characteristics of self-esteem and essential requirements for an enduring relationship. In the extreme form of self-denigration spouses are unable to accept, or retain the care and affection offered from others. These men and women live with the certain conviction of their badness. Desperately anxious to be accepted and loved, they go on reacting to the positive response of others, as if it was not meant for them, or if inescapably directed towards them, it is outwardly accepted and inwardly refused as it meets within their own rejection of themselves.

Repeated requests for affection, urged by those with an enduring sense that nothing can really make them lovable or acceptable, produces a familiar and recurrent marital situation. The complaining partner remonstrates bitterly that the husband or wife neglects them, painting a black picture of the way they are treated. To the astonishment of the marriage counsellor, the bitterly criticized spouse often turns out to be someone who, far from neglecting the partner, has tried everything to reach them and to please them, without success. Every effort has either been repulsed, misconstrued or actually rejected until the spouse, overcome with despair, gives up. At this point the worst fears of neglect are confirmed. When both partners of a marriage have similar feelings about themselves and about each other, there is no basis for a relationship until some modification can be effected. To reach and modify these feelings may require the most protracted counselling.

Frequently what is discovered is an extremely complicated situation. The spouse, who experiences the extremes of bad feelings, desires unconsciously 'to be made good' by the other who is experienced entirely as a parental figure. The latter's inability to change bad feelings into good ones produces fresh waves of fury and guilt which aggravate further the bad identity. Often the partner is expected not only to remove bad feelings, but also to replenish the missing affection of childhood. In other words the husband or wife is required to create a good identity for the first time and to end the intense feelings of deprivation which have persisted since childhood. Needless to say not every partner is competent to fulfil this dual role, but even when they are, there is the final difficulty that when they do act in this way their efforts may be repulsed because they engender in the receiver feelings of dependency and infantility.

A wife summed this up as follows:

'I need a hell of a lot from my husband ... He has to be the father I never had and give me the reassurance I need so badly, but as soon as he begins to do this I feel he treats me like a child which I hate and simply turn nasty and sneer. In fact, poor man, I know he does not mean anything of the sort but all he has to do is to call my name and I expect to be reprimanded. It is stupid, it is silly and if he was not so patient we would have been in the divorce courts years ago because I make life hell for him.'

Unless some insight is reached, there is a relentless pursuit to seek fulfilment and to find a situation in which goodness is experienced. Repeated extra-marital affairs may take place in which the initial hopes are dashed as the same feelings return after a short period. To the disappointment is added the extra guilt of the affair, the possible breaking up of another marriage, the unwanted pregnancy and finally the abortion if the complications go that far. Such traits may, in individual cases, lead to repeated marriages swelling the divorce figures, in which partner after partner is discarded for yet another hope which remains unfulfilled.

Another characteristic of such self-rejection is an intense preoccupation with one's self, paying little attention to the spouse, children or anyone else. Appearance is attended to with meticulous care and a craving for approval and success replaces everything else. This type of behaviour draws the most adverse comments of selfishness, self-centredness, egoism, megalomania, words which are frequently used by the exasperated spouse. Only a close examination reveals that this so-called narcissistic behaviour is the unconscious and sometimes partially concious means by which the person can extricate themselves from the gnawing doubts about their personal value. Unfortunately such behaviour frequently succeeds in alienating the spouse and all others who care genuinely for them without bringing adequate relief to their doubts. An alternative to narcissistic behaviour is the insatiable need to serve and be of use to others. This is behaviour acting on the belief that, if they are not good enough as they are, they will make themselves acceptable by placating, serving and pleasing others. This approach gives a false sense of security and usefulness because underneath there are continuing feelings of badness which can only be assuaged by recurrent appreciation and acknowledgement. Even when these are given liberally they do not extinguish the inner doubts.

Another common solution, mentioned already, is idealization. Idealization is the outcome of concentrating on the positive features of the parents, even endowing them with extra qualities, and the denial of undesirable qualities. This mechanism allows contact to be maintained on the basis of 'I am the bad child, you are the good parent. It is all my fault and I will try to be good to please you.' There is no conscious recognition either of the unreality of the situation or of the inevitable feelings of anger which are deeply repressed. If the idealized parent is not re-appraised he remains the only desirable figure sought after in the spouse.

Idealization implies a high degree of falsification of the original parental situation. In marriage it is difficult to persist with the falsification since the expectations are contradicted by the real behaviour of the spouse. The ensuing tendency of trying to preserve the original relationship opposed and contradicted by the 'idealized' spouse, becomes in the course of time confusing and intolerable. Help is needed to uncover reality, cope with the inevitable feelings of being let down and restore an acceptable identity which no longer needs an idol either for parent or spouse. This restores a sense of equality between the parties which allows a relationship to grow on facts rather than phantasies.

NINE

PSYCHOPATHY

IN the previous three chapters dependence, deprivation and lack of self-esteem were indicated singly or in combination as the three personality traits which most frequently contributed to marital breakdown. While these characteristics are disabling and may indeed destroy a marriage, they may well be confined to close personal relations alone leaving the rest of the personality intact to function in other relationships and at work. These men and women may find it impossible to effect a successful intimate relationship with one particular person but they may do so with somebody else at a later stage and they can certainly sustain less involved relationships.

In 1835 an English physician, Pritchard, coined the term 'moral insanity'. He was the first to describe the personality of a group of people who have drawn increasingly the attention of psychiatrists, penologists and moralists. As the term moral insanity implies, the defect is one which expresses itself particularly in personal conduct, characterized by behaviour which is impulsive, unreliable, extremely limited in its capacity to endure frustration, in the presence of which aggression and violence are easily aroused. The work record is markedly poor, money is squandered leading to fraud, with promiscuity, alcoholism and drug addiction frequently present. The style of behaviour is self-indulgent and destructive. Good intentions are proclaimed and abandoned with such ease that little reliance can be placed on future intentions. The 1959 Mental Health Act defines a 'psychopathic disorder' as a persistent disorder or disability of mind (whether or not including subnormality of intelligence) which results in abnormally aggressive or seriously irresponsible conduct on the part of the patient and requires or is susceptible to treatment. The Act expresses an implicit optimism about the possibilities of treatment which is not shared by the vast majority of psychiatrists, who find such patients extremely resistant to help principally because it is so difficult to form a relationship with them within which therapy can commence or continue. If this obstacle can be overcome, therapy does have some chance of success.

The extreme resistance to therapy is mentioned because the presence of these women and men in a marriage carries a very poor prognosis for its ultimate survival. A few selected case histories have been chosen to illustrate some facets of these disorders which epitomize the ultimate inability to form a stable relationship. A whole book could be devoted to the infinite variety of human disorganization depicted by their life histories.

The psychopathy may be exhibited very early in the marriage, as the first two examples illustrate.

Mary, aged twenty, came from a happy family background in which her two elder brothers were happily married. Her fiancé exhibited no markedly unusual features during their courtship. He was attentive, treated her gently and appeared to be well off financially. The ceremony was in church, both of them being Protestants. He admitted that he did not take religion seriously but that he was prepared to meet her wishes in this matter. The day before the ceremony he appeared anxious which she put down to pre-wedding nerves. At the wedding ceremony he was intoxicated, an event which took her completely by surprise causing her and her family a great deal of embarrassment. He just managed to negotiate the celebrations afterwards but insisted on leaving as soon as possible. On the way to the car he apologized profusely to her and put it down to 'nerves'. After about an hour in the car on their way to Scotland where they were to spend their honeymoon, he stopped the car by a telephone kiosk and made a mysterious telephone call. He returned to the car and explained to her, once again with profuse apologies, that he had forgotten something, ('He never told me what it was.') and had to return to his flat. He drove her to the nearest hotel and left her. He did not return that night but rang her up explaining that he was held up and she would have to stay in the hotel. She discovered later that he had spent the night with a previous girl friend. He returned the next day with a story of a broken-down car. He continued to apologize and, despite mounting suspicion, she accepted his apologies. They had a happy honeymoon, with satisfactory sexual relations. On their return, the relationship deteriorated within a matter of weeks. The second night after their return he did not come home.

'He told me he was called away suddenly on business. I began to be frightened. He told me there was nothing to worry about. The next week he asked me for some money which I gave him. He came home drunk that night and, in a shattering outburst, he told me that he did not love me, he never wanted to marry me and asked me to get out ... My protests were met with physical violence which left me in no doubt of the urgent necessity to leave.'

In the inevitable legal proceedings her husband was found to have served a prison sentence for theft and to have had over fifty jobs. At the time of their marriage he was in debt to the tune of several hundred pounds. Her final comment was, 'I just had no idea how I found myself in such a mess. I was taken in completely by his kindness and gentleness.'

In the second case events were not so dramatic and there were some warning signs beforehand. The engagement was broken once by the husband and his wife knew that he had a tendency towards heavy drinking and short temper. After twelve months of marriage the wife could stand it no longer. The first night of their honeymoon was a terrible shock. 'He treated me like an animal.' His sexual demands became impossible. 'He asked me to do things which were disgusting and if I didn't agree he knocked me about. Since he did not go out to work he had plenty of time for one thing. We hadn't been married more than a few months when I caught him carrying on with the girl next door. Drink, knocking me about and that girl finished any love I had for him.'

The next couple illustrate the emergence of psychopathy early in a marriage which nevertheless survived for six years. Like the previous couple, the background of the spouses was working class. All went well for the first six months. Then she conceived and, from the moment he knew she was pregnant, his behaviour changed. He wanted her to have an abortion which she refused. Reluctantly he accepted the baby but kept late hours, drank to excess and occasionally struck her with little provocation. After the child was born he became increasingly aggressive, started changing his job every few months and there was financial hardship. His response to her repeated requests for help was to force her to go out as a prostitute. 'I must have been mad . . . I hated the whole thing but in some stupid way I was still in love with him.' She was caught and fined and for a while he returned to regular work. Shortly after this he had an accident which prevented him from working. During this period she became pregnant again. This time he insisted on an abortion which she had. He did not return to regular work and at this point they parted. She came back after six weeks but the situation did not improve. He was caught housebreaking and put on probation. He broke his probation and on the second occasion was sent to prison. When he was discharged from prison he deserted her.

Psychopathy is not confined to men or to any particular socio-economic group. A girl of nineteen had been deserted by her mother when she was two. She remembered her father leaving her with a priest who in turn placed her in an orphanage run by nuns. She did not complain about her treatment except that there were too many children for individual attention. She left the orphanage when she was sixteen. She had had fourteen jobs by the time she was eighteen and then she drifted into Soho. She became a prostitute and a drug addict and finally found her way into a mental hospital as a result of an attempted suicide. There she struck up an acquaintance with a youth of eighteen who paid her a great deal of attention. 'For the first time in my life I thought someone really cared for me . . .' They married soon after their discharge. There were difficulties with housing, money, and work for both of them. Despite the help they received, she drifted back to prostitution and drugs. Within six months of marriage she had left her husband.

The final example concerns an intelligent and gifted man who came from a home that appeared to lavish attention and love on him. His wife was the girl next door. They started going around together when they were sixteen. He felt all along that he would marry her but that he was not 'in love'. He went away for his military service, during which period he had innumerable affairs. During his leaves he resumed his relationship with his girl-friend and married her. When he left the forces he found it difficult to settle down and he turned down several jobs. Finally, he entered the field of commercial art where he was a success. He gradually developed a thriving business. At home he continued to remain restless and discontented. He was unfaithful to his wife on several occasions, paying little attention to her or to his children. After eight years of marriage he disappeared. There was no contact with him for several months while his business came to a halt and his family suffered severe financial and emotional strain. He was traced to a hospital where he had been admitted with loss of memory. On recovery, he admitted the impossibility of carrying on with his wife and felt the only answer was to get away. He had worked as a casual labourer moving from place to place. He had no desire to pick up the threads of his work, no genuine desire to return to his wife but he felt very guilty about his children.

Little is known about the causes of such behaviour but it is very likely that 'psychopathy' is the end result of a multiplicity of factors in which genetically predisposed individuals are further disabled by environments where the rudiments of social and personal relationships are barely established. Indeed their family background is often, though not invariably, loaded with the usual adverse factors of broken homes and absent or unreliable parental figures. The presence of such a person in a marriage frequently leads to an impossible situation where marriage exists in name only, the relationship being otherwise conducted on the basis of unilateral or mutual abuse, aggression and total disorganization, leading to frequent separations and ultimately to divorce.

It is very doubtful if persons suffering from such grave defects in their personality are capable of making valid vows in this state. Their previous life history gives ample evidence of their inconsistency, unreliability and inability to accept responsibility for their promises and/or actions. The severe impairment may be difficult to demonstrate because at a superficial examination or on casual acquaintance there are no obvious psychological deficits. On the contrary, there may well be a deceptive charm and a convincing manner, made good use of by confidence tricksters. Emotional instability and the utter inadequacy of the individual is only demonstrated when the life history is taken as a whole along with a dismal work record, previous complete inability to form anything but casual and fleeting acquaintanceships and an emotional indifference which can amount to sheer callousness.

TEN

SEXUAL DIFFICULTIES

PERHAPS no cause has been so widely canvassed as responsible for marital disharmony than sexual dissatisfaction. This is not surprising since marriage remains the main outlet for the fulfilment of sexual needs and sexual intercourse is a constant reminder of the closeness and unity of the partners. Persistent disappointment in sexual relations is not only a personal deprivation but also one that is no longer congruent with the expectations of our day.

In what proportion of couples is sexual dissatisfaction directly responsible for marital breakdown? There are very few marriages in serious difficulty without sexual problems, so it is important to assess the specific contribution of sexual failure *per se*. This is extremely difficult to do because there is an intimate link between the total relationship and the quality of the sexual experience. Nevertheless some facts are available.

In a study of 739 couples who were married in this country between 1950 and 1959, 48·2 per cent reported adjustment difficulties but only 3·2 referred to sexual ones.[2] Even more significant is the fact that out of the thirty-five couples (5 per cent) who separated or contemplated separation only one informant reported sexual difficulties. This study was concerned with the overall incidence of sexual disorder but did not distinguish the contribution of sexual orgasm, particularly for the woman. Male orgasm is almost invariably achieved in all cases where erection and intercourse is possible but this is not the case of the wife. Wallin [36] who was the co-author of a detailed study of 1,000 engaged couples in the United States, examined these same couples some three to five years later, paying particular attention to the presence of an orgasm as a condition of woman's enjoyment of sexual intercourse. He came to the conclusion that although there was a high positive correlation between orgasm frequency and the extent to which women obtained relief from sexual desire, orgasm was neither necessary nor a sufficient condition for woman's sexual relief.

In this and other studies as well as in clinical experience there is ample evidence to suggest that sexual orgasm is neither essential for sexual relief nor is its absence an inevitable contribution to marital breakdown. Sexual intercourse itself may be completely absent and a marriage remain happy. This is not to underrate the importance of the physical exchange in marriage but to emphasize that successful orgastic experience is not an essential pre-requisite for marital happiness. One eminent worker[37] has summarized succinctly the situation: 'It is necessary to make it clear from the start that an orgasm is not a panacea for all marital woe and that sex can cause as much trouble when intercourse itself is physiologically successful as when it is unsuccessful. I have never seen a marriage made or broken by sex alone, except in the case of frank perversions.' This assertion can be backed by clinical experience and it demands an examination of the characteristics and significance of the sexual act.

The sexual act is the confrontation of two people in the most delicate human exchange where two bodies form but one part of the complex physical, psychological and spiritual union of love-making. It is important to consider these three components separately.

Knowledge of sexual anatomy and technique of sexual intercourse are of course necessary and, in practice, a couple, who are perfectly attuned in every other respect, may fail to achieve successful intercourse through sheer ignorance of anatomical knowledge and skill in performing the act. Here help is very rewarding and there are couples whose marriage can be transformed in this way.

The vast majority of couples who are experiencing sexual difficulties do so after intercourse has actually been achieved. Local disease such as infection, trauma or neoplasm has to be excluded, for this accounts for a tiny minority of the difficulties. There is left the biological and psychological differences between men and women in their capacity to obtain an orgasm.

The innate capacity to respond sexually in both men and women does vary considerably. Kinsey,[38] writing on the innate capacity for orgasm in woman, says:

For instance, the exceedingly rapid response of certain females who are able to reach orgasm within a matter of seconds from the time they are first stimulated, and the remarkable ability of some females to reach orgasm repeatedly within a short period of time, are capacities which most other individuals could not conceivably acquire through training, childhood experience or any sort of psychiatric therapy. Similarly, it seems reasonable to believe that at least some of the females who are slower in their response are not equipped anatomically or physiologically as those who respond more rapidly. Unfortunately we do not know yet enough about the anatomy and physiology of sexual response to understand the exact origins of such individual variation.'

One of the many factors concerned with female response is the length of time the penis is in the vagina prior to ejaculation. Results from a recently published study[39] indicate that there is a tendency for higher orgasm rates to be associated with greater duration of intromission. Where intromission is under one minute, only about a quarter of the wives achieve orgasm: and beyond eleven minutes orgasm is achieved by between three-fifths to two-thirds of wives. The fifty per cent rate achieved by intromission ranging from one to eleven minutes is suggestive that an all-or-none response is triggered off through a minimum of one minute penetration. These findings are in complete agreement with the common clinical finding that men who find it difficult to sustain more than a brief period of intromission fail regularly to please their wives. The failure to sustain erection for longer periods is due to a combination of factors such as reduced libido, fatigue and very frequently anxiety and possibly other unknown factors.

Another factor associated with the woman's response is the timing of the act in relation to the phase in her monthly cycle. Kinsey's[40] results, supported by other studies,[41] are in conflict with studies in lower species. In the sub-human species sexual desire in the female is at its highest at the time of ovulation, that is when she is likely to conceive. Kinsey reported that women experience maximal sexual desire before and after menstruation with a low level during the middle of the cycle when ovulation and possible conception occur. Failure to appreciate this pattern may lead to a lot of misunderstanding. The husband may feel hurt and angry at the indifference of his wife which is incomprehensible as there are no analogous variations in him and the wife may become anxious about her inability to please and be satisfied.

To these biological variations the psychological factors need to be added. Sexual intercourse is the focal point of a union which has been preceded by a relationship. Only intercourse with a prostitute requires no previous or subsequent relationship and this is certainly one of its attractive features for those men and women who cannot achieve or tolerate anything more intense than a fleeting or casual exchange. In marriages each act is preceded by the accumulated interpersonal contact of weeks, months and years. If the passage of time smoothes the problems, leads to mutual fulfilment and increases closeness, sexual intercourse will become a recurrent pleasure even though orgasm for the wife is not always possible. If, on the other hand, there are personality problems producing tension, hostility and fear, it would be most surprising if these feelings failed to influence this most sensitive experience. The wife can express these various feelings by refusal, indifference and failure to appreciate her husband's effort. A couple who had sought help stated that the wife never refused her husband but she had driven him to distraction by looking at the ceiling and never at him. Inquiry revealed that during intercourse she looked for and counted cobwebs and insects on the walls and ceiling! Such dutiful compliance gives way to refusal and the following piece of imaginative writing summarizes the complaints of many husbands all over the world.

'To my ever-loving wife,

During the past year I have attempted to seduce you 365 times. I succeeded thirty-six times. This averages once every ten days, the following is a list of excuses made on the unsuccessful occasions:

We will wake the children	7	The baby is crying	18
It's too hot	15	Watched late show	7
It's too cold	3	Watched early show	5
Too tired	19	Mudpack on	12
It's too late	16	Grease on face	6
It's too early	9	Reading Sunday paper	10
Pretending to sleep	33	You are too drunk	9
Windows open, neighbours will hear	3	We have company in the next room	7
Your back ached	16	Your parents were staying with us	5
Toothache	2	My parents were staying with us	5
Headache	26	Is that all you ever think about?	105
Giggling fit	2		
I've had too much	4		
Not in the mood	21		

Do you think you could improve our record this coming year?

Your ever-loving husband

Despite popular belief negative feelings are not the sole prerogative of the wife. The husband too can inflict his anger by taking no pains with the love-making, by insisting on relief without concern for his wife's response and, ultimately by not having sexual intercourse at all. This ultimate refusal communicates the maximum rejection to his wife, instilling at the same time anxiety and suspicion that he is finding his pleasure elsewhere.

The current preoccupation with sexual gratification and the previous obsession with procreation have tended to distract attention from one of the principal features of the act, which is the powerful reassurance it gives to the couple at all times but particularly during special periods of need, that each wants and is prepared to accept the other unconditionally. This is an unconditional acceptance which is not in evidence elsewhere in life, except in the early and unspoiled relationship between the baby and its mother.

Not only do the spouses act as powerful agents of mutual reassurance but they also encourage the fullest growth of each other's sexual identity. Nothing makes a man or woman more so than the certain knowledge that they are wanted and appreciated by each other.

When self-esteem is low and confidence lacking the sexual act becomes more than a reassurance, it becomes an urgent therapy, perhaps one of the most powerful forms of treatment the spouses can carry out for one another. But here the difficulties emerge. The frequency of the male desire is resented by the wife, who complains bitterly that her spouse is inhuman, a brute, interested in only one thing, and caring for nothing else. The husband's own persistent physical needs are interpreted as unreasonable, excessive and cruel. If the wife shares the same psychological difficulties as her husband, and the presence of assortative mating encourages this, her inability to extract the same reassurance from the sexual act as her husband makes her unwilling to go on giving herself in a way that produces little gratification or diminution of her anxieties. Behind the common complaint by the wife of the husband's inordinate sexual demands there lies frequently the conscious or unconscious resentment that her needs are not being met, making her feel used and exploited rather than loved.

These physiological and psychological factors need to be implemented by sexual education which varies with the social background of the couple. Sexual education is vital. Silence, ignorance and active condemnation may leave the grown-up man with a sexual drive separated from affection and the woman with an experience of sex as a mere irrelevance. A sexual awakening needs more than a biological drive, it requires also a social awareness of its significance. Kinsey[42] demonstrated the importance of a rising level of sexual education by his findings which showed that married women who had never responded to the point of orgasm in the first year of marriage were 33 per cent amongst those born before 1900 but only 23 per cent amongst those born after 1909. These differences persisted after fifteen years of marriage. Kinsey also found that wives with high education level and those who came from an upper social class had persistently greater coital response. This observation that lower-class husbands and wives are less likely to find sexual relations gratifying than couples of the higher socio-economic groups has been confirmed in other studies.[43] Lee Rainwater[44] studied this phenomenon further and found that within the lower socio-economic groups there is a further division. Following the work of Elizabeth Bott,[45] he divided married couples into those who showed a high degree of participation in each other's activities, which he designated jointly organized, as against the highly segregated whose work at home, visiting and recreation are marked by a high degree of separatedness. The findings strongly suggest that it is in the highly segregated couples that the wives are negative towards sexual relations. Since the wife's interest in sex tends to be more heavily dependent upon a sense of interpersonal closeness and gratification in her total relationship with her husband, it is very difficult for her to find gratification in sex in the context of a highly segregated role relationship.[44] Such social influences may of course be overriden by other factors, such as the intrinsic capacity of the wife. In their book *Patterns of Marriage*[28] dealing with working-class marriage, Slater and Woodside give examples of a very high sexual response in the case of Mrs P.

Mrs P., aged twenty-six, says sex is 'perfect'; she has been married nearly five years, has intercourse most nights, and sometimes by day as well. She has orgasm every time. He is a perfect lover. She is highly sexed and finds the enforced abstinence 'terrible'. Sex is 'the only thing in life sometimes. He need only hold my hand and I want him.'

Finally to these physiological, psychological and social factors must be added the duration and the quality of the marrage itself. Several studies had found that the sexual response of the wife improves with the duration of marriage. Kinsey[46] reports that nearly fifty per cent of the married women in his sample experienced orgasm within the first month of marriage. This had risen to 75 per cent by the end of the first year. After fifteen years of marriage only 10 per cent of his sample had never experienced an orgasm.

Gebhard,[47] who was a co-worker of Kinsey, extended the original research and discovered that the quality of the marriage influenced the wife's response. In a sample of 8,000 women he found that in the very happy marriages only 4·4 per cent of them did not experience orgasm compared with 19 per cent in the very unhappy group. Clark and Wallin,[48] carrying out similar studies, confirm that wives whose marriage is consistently positive are likely to be increasingly responsive sexually. Increased sexual response may however be halted and, indeed, deterioration set in, if the quality of the marriage suffers.

In dealing with these various factors influencing the sexual act, the term 'frigidity' has been deliberately avoided. The term means, of course, a reduced or absent sexual desire in the woman. There is a danger in using this term of describing a fixed entity and a defect which belongs entirely to the woman. Neither of the propositions is correct. Women are capable of responding differently to different men in different situations. Even more important, every sexual act represents the *combined* response of the couple which is governed by all the variables mentioned in this chapter. The majority of persistently serious sexual complaints are the end result of personality conflicts manifesting themselves in this extremely sensitive area. Sexual dissatisfaction, in turn, aggravates the relationship thus setting up a vicious circle which may end in marital breakdown.

ELEVEN

SEXUAL DIFFICULTIES (continued)

NON-CONSUMMATION, FAILURE OF COITUS AND SEXUAL DEVIATIONS

THE previous chapter was devoted to an examination of the sexual act without reference to the rare but serious problems when intercourse cannot be performed at all. Until recently this was considered entirely the problem of the husband, whose impotence or markedly poor sexual performance was thought to be the sole root of the problem. The husband's total and persistent inability to obtain an erection appeared superficially to place the problem firmly on his side but even here the wife's attitude can make a marked difference. In those couples where the husband does get an erection but cannot successfully penetrate, the wife's behaviour is vital. Non-consummation may be present initially and temporarily or continue indefinitely in some marriages, and in these cases provides one of the grounds for nullity. The number of marriages that are dissolved on these grounds are a fraction of total dissolutions, in fact less than 2 per cent of all the marriages that reach the courts are dissolved for this reason. Nor does every non-consummation manage to reach the courts. I have known happy non-consummated marriages that have lasted various periods up to twenty years. In these couples the absence of sexual intercourse is mutually agreed upon, the subject is left untouched and the couple proceed to form a satisfactory non-sexual union. Where, however, one or both partners find such a situation intolerable, they may seek help.

Either spouse may take such initiative and the presentation of the difficulty is couched either non-critically or in accusatory terms depending on the quality of the relationship. If the relationship is good, there is a simple acknowledgement that despite considerable effort they have not been able to consummate the marriage. When the relationship is unsatisfactory the non-consummation will be interpreted in an accusatory fashion and the partner blamed for his or her failure. The 'causes' put forward are stereotyped. The husband is considered too big or the wife too small, he is ignorant and has hurt her too much, he can't get near her. Gross physical defects need eliminating, such as absence of or deformed vagina, neurological disease, or anatomical deformity in the case of the man. Other instances will be found when sexual instruction and education have been totally lacking and the couple are not aware of the rudiments of anatomy and position for intercourse. With the necessary explanation and help consummation may be achieved speedily. Finally there are the numerous couples in whom psychological difficulties predominate.

Some wives have not reached a sufficient genital level of sexual maturation to allow penetration. After a few desultory attempts the exchange is abandoned and the wife withdraws from a most painful experience for which she was totally unprepared.

A pretty, vivacious twenty-one-year-old clerk came with her husband aged twenty-two for help. He described their courtship in which she appeared to him overwhelmingly attractive, and sexually seductive. She confirmed this and acknowledged that she had done everything she could to stimulate him until their wedding. During the honeymoon she accepted all his caresses until sexual intercourse itself from which she withdrew completely. She appeared eager to solve her problem and agreed to come to the clinic to learn how to relax and be instructed in the use of dilators. She came faithfully week after week and went through the procedures mechanically and very clearly emotionally uninvolved. Further discussion revealed her total repudiation of that part of her body. Finally she admitted that she did not want to know anything about her genitalia or intercourse. She did not want to be a woman, it was fun being a girl. All she wanted was to remain as a good friend of her husband. He continued to live with her and reported her unceasing flirtation with him which inevitably came to an abrupt halt when intercourse was approached. It became evident that she was functioning psychologically at a pre-genital level sexually and could not advance from that position. Her bewildered husband gradually came to realize this and sought dissolution.

The most frequent pattern is that of the woman who wants to have sexual intercourse but is intensely apprehensive thereby causing marked physical tension, which makes it impossible for the husband to penetrate. There are many reasons for such anxiety. The fear of being hurt is common and the wife is usually a sensitive person easily threatened by the prospect of pain or discomfort. Actual physical trauma in that area in the past may have occurred. Injections, enemas, catheterisation, treatment for worms, and so on may have left painful memories. More often there are more complex psycho-sexual difficulties such as the fear of becoming pregnant, of losing control, of permitting a legally sanctioned but previously experienced taboo, and occasionally the resuscitation of incest phantasies. The initial sexual act may have been mismanaged by an inexperienced husband causing the re-emergence of deep-seated fears of being attacked and irreparably hurt.

In all these couples a vicious circle is set up in which fear and apprehension further aggravate the muscular tension, making each fresh attempt more painful until a state is reached when no further attempts are possible.

The situation is additionally complicated because the wife's predisposition to such conscious or unconscious anxieties leads her to choose the type of man who is gentle, equally anxious and does not appear likely to make heavy sexual demands on her. This, in fact, is a hindrance in the management of non-consummation, because the husband's tolerance and apparent kindness have not only allowed the problem to continue for a long time before treatment is sought but, if his own sexual needs and capacity are limited, there is no particular hurry to change the situation. When he does attempt to achieve consummation, his gentleness is a handicap because he colludes with his wife in her easily activated painful response and is not prepared to be assertive and overcome gently her resistance.

Help is needed not only for the wife but also for the husband, emphasizing the point that in practice all sexual problems involve both partners who need to be familiarized with their own specific roles and contributions. The successful outcome of treatment depends as much on the nature of the problems as the couple's desire to overcome their difficulties. High motivation on the part of both partners is vital. After the mechanics and psychological significance of the sexual act are explained, patience, gentleness and encouragement are needed to learn how to relax. In uncomplicated cases the treatment is often successful. There are couples however where the intrinsic limitations cannot be overcome. The survival of such a marriage will then depend on their mutual ability to fulfil each other's needs non-sexually.

Impotence and premature ejaculation are conditions related exclusively to male sexual performance. They range from complete loss of erection to various degrees of partial insufficiency, in which the commonest difficulty is the inability to sustain the erection for a sufficiently long period to penetrate or, having done so, to sustain the erection sufficiently long enough to give the wife satisfaction. Associated with insufficient erectile power is premature ejaculation in which the male climax is reached rapidly, outside the vagina or just after penetration. (Nonetheless this may still allow the deposit of sufficient semen close enough to the vagina for fertilization.)

Impotence caused by failure of erection was found by Kinsey[49] to be present in ·4 per cent of males under twenty-five rising steadily with age to 6·7 per cent at fifty and 75 per cent of more or less impotence by the age of eighty. Impotence is the end result of constitutional, physiological limitations, disease (amongst which hormone deficiencies, diabetes, depression and local or general disease of the nervous system play a prominent part) and psychological difficulties. The latter include failure of psycho-sexual maturation, excessive proneness to anxiety and overt and covert sexual deviations of which homosexuality is the commonest.

The psycho-sexual development requires the presence of a minimum identification with a male figure in childhood, normally the father, whose role and behaviour is free from ambiguities and sufficiently positive to be repeated in the adult life of the son. The absence of such a figure, coupled with the presence of a dominating or over-protective mother, hinders the growth of a male identity. Sometimes there is a general failure of emotional growth which includes sexuality, on other occasions the defect is confined to the sexual field.

The outcome frequently depends on the attitude of the wife. Her support, coupled with a positive physical encouragement, can turn a mediocre response to a much improved one. Failure with one woman can on occasions be converted to success with another who is able to arouse a greater degree of sexual drive, diminish anxieties and inspire confidence in performance. The reverse occurs when the overall relationship is unsatisfactory and the poverty of the performance is the subject of criticism or derision. Such criticisms have a discouraging and humiliating effect driving the failure more deeply, converting a partial failure to one that is complete.

This is a situation that can set a trap for the couple. The failure of the man is too obvious to be missed. The wife attaches her hostility on this and demands that the husband should receive treatment, placing on him full responsibility for the situation and protecting herself from her own problems. He cannot disclaim failure, accepts the responsibility and is full of guilt. No amount of help given to the husband is likely to succeed unless the wife becomes acquainted with her own difficulties and she ceases to project all her own problems on her spouse. Only when the mutual obstacles and hindrances of fear and hostility are removed is there any hope of success. When this is achieved at the psychological level additional help may be derived from drugs which diminish anxiety and tension.

SEXUAL DEVIATIONS

Sexual deviation has received different definitions. Sir Norwood East[50] defined it as 'A persistently indulged sexual activity in which complete satisfaction is sought and obtained without the necessity of heterosexual intercourse.' It may be indulged in reality or in phantasy and the crucial factor is its persistent quality. Such a definition is acceptable for clinical psychiatric practice but is far too restricting in considering the role it plays in marital pathology. In marriage it is not only the failure of normal heterosexual activity which is damaging. Every single episode of sexual deviation confronts the wife or the husband with an event that has marked psychological and social overtones. The damage is inflicted more by the shock and surprise that one's partner is capable of such behaviour than by the consequences of the act itself. Here, even more than elsewhere, the future of the marriage will depend on the quality of the relationship.

The incidence of sexual deviations in marriages is not known, for only a fraction reach the light of day in courts or a marriage counselling service. Even so one comprehensive study of 8,000 male married patients at the Maudsley hospital showed that there were eighty-nine men with sexual deviations, of whom eleven were involved in separation, divorce or extramarital relations. The incidence of sexual deviations amongst women leading to marital breakdown is extremely rare. In this study there was only one woman with this condition whose marriage had broken down.[51] This study suggests that the part played by sexual deviations in marital breakdown is small.

The incidence of exclusive male homosexuality is, according to Kinsey,[52] of the order of 4 per cent and therefore in magnitude surpasses all other problems in this category. The exclusive homosexual presents few difficulties as far as marriage is concerned because heterosexual activities are neither desired nor practised. There is, however, a group of men with undoubted homosexual propensities whose intensity is low enough to allow some heterosexual contact ultimately leading to marriage. The overall incidence of homosexuality in married men is not known but its wide prevalence makes it undoubtedly the leading sexual deviation likely to be encountered in marital pathology.

Men in their thirties or forties who, for social or religious reasons, feel they must marry, persevere in their limited heterosexual interests in the hope that marriage will either cure their homosexual leanings or will prove to them that their fears were not justified. This approach may be foolishly encouraged by advice received at the hands of well-meaning friends or the priest. After the marriage, sexual intercourse may take place once or on a few occasions and then will become increasingly impossible and unacceptable. The husband departs from the bedroom leaving behind a bewildered and hurt wife. After a few weeks or months the marriage will have come to a complete standstill at the physical level. In some instances it will not even reach this stage, and some of the problems associated with non-consummation involve marked homosexual tendencies on the part of the husband, and sometimes, but much more rarely, the wife.

Homosexuality need not manifest itself in this clear manner at the beginning of marriage. The mixture of homo- and heterosexual tendencies may allow sufficient heterosexual activity to raise a family while still maintaining homosexual needs sufficiently powerful to demand satisfaction. This desire may be curbed by religious motivation, fear of social censure or hurting the wife and children but its presence continuously threatens the marriage. Under stress the husband may give way to homosexual contact. If the wife is not aware of the incident, he then has to live with the constant anxiety of exposure with its attendant personal and family disgrace and, up to recently, the sanctions of the law, which applied even to consenting adults. When the wife is familiar with the situation, the future of the marriage depends, as in all these situations, on her attitude.

Lesbianism presents a much smaller problem for, when marriage has been undertaken, the homosexual needs can be satisfied without attracting the same complications. This is not possible however if the attraction of another woman is experienced simultaneously with increasing hatred towards the husband, in which case the marriage breaks down.

The essence of *sadism* or *masochism* is the fusion of emotional gratification, particularly of a sexual nature, with behaviour which, consciously or unconsciously, either inflicts or seeks pain and suffering. This suffering does not need to be physical, although it is there that the gross manifestations of the psychological anomalies exhibit themselves. Far more often the suffering is communicated through non-physical means. Minor forms of sado-masochism may be present in a marriage without either of the spouses being aware of it. Quarrels and arguments, with their attendant reconciliations, can be occasions in which minor suffering is inflicted and received, from which the couple may get an unrecognized pleasure, sufficiently important to ensure that the occasions are repeated, without threatening the survival of the marriage. Real difficulties begin when the necessity to inflict or receive pain is such that only in the presence of physical, emotional or moral suffering can the person feel that his needs are met satisfactorily. Here there may be unconscious collusions in which, unknown to each other, the characteristics of the spouses are such that the sadistic needs in one are reciprocated by the masochistic requirements in the other. These marriages are always precarious, because the relationship is based on a world of infantile needs and fantasies. The couple represent and symbolize to each other key parental figures with whom pockets of infantile behaviour are being relived. The dangers are two-fold. First, as long as the behaviour is a standing contradiction between the adult realities and infantile needs of the couple, it creates tension and stress. Secondly, with the passage of time, the inevitable maturation brings about changes in the emotional needs. Unless these are roughly of the same degree, differential demands will make the position untenable for one or both spouses.

If sexual relations can only be achieved in the presence of gross sado-masochistic behaviour, the chances of such a relationship surviving are slim, unless treatment produces the necessary amelioration.

Transvestism is a rare sexual anomaly in which one partner, usually the husband, derives sexual satisfaction from wearing the clothes, particularly the underclothes, of the opposite sex, frequently those of his wife. These difficulties have to be clearly distinguished from homosexuality, where the love-object is a person of the same sex and which does not involve any change in the characteristic features of appearance of one's own sex. The desire to dress in feminine clothes and to indulge in sexual activity in this way is caused by the failure to adopt the male role and its objectives. The man not only wishes to dress in feminine clothes but a good deal more of his emotional development has failed to accept the male role, and consequently the marriage experiences difficulties in fields other than the sexual one. Without effective treatment such marriages in their extreme form are not likely to survive, being the very antithesis of the male-female complementarity.

Fetishism is a condition characterized by the replacement of the normal sexual activity with a person of the opposite sex, or in the case of homosexuality a person of the same sex, by parts belonging to that person and/or, in the extreme cases, by inanimate objects totally disconnected with the person. Common fetishes are articles of female clothing, rubber, shoes, mackintosh and furs. It is an almost entirely male difficulty which in its extreme form makes marriage impossible. There are, however, a number of men who, while able to have normal sexual relations, seek its intensification through phantasy or through the wife wearing fetish objects. The wife's toleration of such demands will decide the future of the marriage.

Voyeurism and exhibitionism are almost exclusively male deviations. Exhibitionism is characterized by the exposure of the genitalia to the opposite sex outside the context of the sexual act. Voyeurism is a deviation in which sexual pleasure is derived from watching women undressing and sexual intercourse taking place. Exhibitionism lends itself to apprehension and conviction especially when young children are involved. Of the 6,161 sexual offenders found guilty in 1959, one third were exhibitionists.[53] Thus to the suffering caused by the presence of such a defect is added that of conviction and imprisonment of the husband, an aggravating factor not found in other deviations except homosexuality.

These sexual anomalies are generally interpreted as remnants of infantile sources of gratification persisting in adult life. The present form of treatment is either by psychotherapy or aversion therapy. The impact that these conditions have on marriage depends on the quality of the marital relationship. If this is harmonious and the needs of each other are met with a minimum of satisfaction at other levels, then the deviation becomes a common problem shared and worked out in the best possible way with or without treatment. If difficulties exist at other levels then the deviation becomes a convenient vehicle on which the other unresolved issues are unloaded.

TWELVE

BIRTH CONTROL AND THE SIZE OF THE FAMILY

THE economic, social and psychological problems associated with the size of the family hold pre-eminence in current discussions on marriage. The large family and its difficulties is the issue most frequently discussed but, with regard to marital disharmony, it is the childless marriage that has a prominent association with divorce. All studies concur that the childless marriage runs a risk, well above the average, of ending in divorce. Jacobson's[54] careful analysis of the information available in 1948 in the United States gives the childless couple a rate of divorce which is double that of those with children. Rowntree[4] in this country shows that infertile couples parting have as much as a five-fold increase in the age group up to nineteen compared with fertile couples and this marked disparity is shown in the twenty to twenty-five group as well.

Thus statistics appear to show convincingly that childless marriages are more likely to end in divorce. The word 'appear' is used because these findings have been criticized severely by Monahan[55] and others who state that in the final analysis marital stability may have no general relationship to childbearing. (Such contradictory findings and views are not infrequent in this very young science of studying marriage and the family and here, as elsewhere, early conclusions have to be continuously tested by reliable data which are hard to obtain.) Monahan's criticisms are based on a review of previous research in which he points out that basic definitions of a child vary in the many studies which use terms such as minor, dependent, living children, and so on, without defining their terms, making conclusions hard to compare. He attacks Jacobson for not differentiating the time of divorce from the time of separation of the couple, since fertility is determined by the latter. He also points out that in desertion and cases of nonsupport, children are much more in evidence and, since some of these couples will end in divorce, this may alter the picture. Furthermore, some religious and racial groups do not make use of divorce but rather of separation, thus making the ranks of the former unrepresentative. All these points have to be assessed carefully before the original findings can be shown to be conclusive.

Burgess and Wallin[56] go further:

Even if the statistics showing a relationship between childlessness and the permanence of marriage were not open to the above and other criticisms they would still not prove that children are a deterrent to divorce. The greater incidence of childlessness among couples who divorce could be due to the possibility that couples who are dissatisfied with their marriage tend to put off having children lest this worsen their relationships, or because they anticipate getting a divorce. The fact that the divorce rate declines with increase in the number of children is consistent with this interpretation. Couples who continue to have children are not likely to be thinking about getting a divorce. Furthermore, it may be that the kinds of persons who do not desire children tend to be those who are prone to be unsuccessful in marriage and consequently more likely to divorce.

Who are the people who do not desire to have children? Reference has been made to marriages in which there is a homosexual partner and to the non-consummated marriages; these people have their own distinctive difficulties. There are others who do not fall into these categories. There is, for example, the group in which the development of the husband or wife is not sufficiently advanced to face the problems presented by a new life, and they keep putting off pregnancy. Usually the reasons offered are the common ones such as inadequate accommodation, finance or the desire of the wife to continue her work. However, as soon as the current problem is rectified some other reason is picked upon. To such couples child-bearing is an intolerable conscious or unconscious anxiety which cannot be faced by the wife and an impossible challenge for the husband. These anxieties are present in people who are likely to be vulnerable in other aspects of the relationship, putting the marriage into the less stable group. It is frequently stated that children bind parents together in a common goal and purpose and this is true, but before this process can take place there must be sufficient psychological and emotional resources in the couple to bring about this cohesion even in the most elementary form. The absence of this minimal ability may be manifested in the complete unwillingness of the couple to pursue the task of procreation.

Miss P. was twenty-three, a practising Roman Catholic who wished to marry a Protestant. He was quite willing to undertake the necessary course of instruction and make the required promises. They were both university students, intellectually suited to one another. Miss P. sought advice prior to the wedding because she felt that under no circumstances was she prepared to have a child. She knew that this was contrary to the purpose of marriage as her faith taught her and indeed as she felt marriage ought to be. Her fiancé was willing to comply with her wishes but she was not satisfied with her attitude. Closer psychological examination revealed a deep-rooted antipathy to the idea of children, associated with her own marked emotional unpreparedness to suffer any restriction of her freedom of activities. Her childhood had been extremely unhappy and her marriage expressed her need to feel close to someone she could turn to for help and support but she did not feel that she could cope with a child, the sight of whom in other people's homes filled her with disgust and hatred. She had not established her own separate role in life, either in terms of her identity or emotional security, and a child would have been an appalling threat to her own survival. She was offered help and advised against immediate marriage which would have had little chance of surviving if birth prevention had been unsuccessful.

There is, of course, a clear-cut difference between the couples who desire a family and cannot have one, variously calculated at between eight and ten per cent of all marriages, and the couples who cannot undertake this task because of their personality difficulties.

Another way of examining the problem is to determine the overtly expressed attitude of the couple to having children.

Are children desired or not? Two studies already referred to in the book by Burgess and Wallin indicate that the attitude to having children is an important indicator for future marital happiness. Couples who have a positive attitude and desire children are clearly more likely to make a successful marriage. They conclude that it is attitude rather than actual size of the family that is important for marital success. The evidence is not conclusive and experience suggests that there is a limit for an individual couple beyond which additions to the family create a serious situation, but a positive and welcoming attitude is a powerful and valuable aid to support the couple in the extra difficulties created by a larger than average size family.

Children are one of the main purposes of marriage but the size and timing of the family have been coming increasingly under the influence of *birth control.* Various studies, both in Great Britain and the United States, indicate that between seventy and eighty per cent of married couples have at some time used various methods, predominantly male ones, to control fertility,[57,58]

The reasons for this widespread resort to birth control are many. The advances of medicine have greatly reduced infant mortality. In 1911 the total infant mortality (death under one year) was 129·4 per 1,000 live births; by 1960 it had dropped to 21·8 per 1,000 live births.[59] Miscarriages still take place but nearly eighty-five per cent of pregnancies can be expected to result in live births.[60] Advances in medicine save lives which then have to be fed, clothed and housed. There are currently many arguments about the optimum size of the world population, but whatever the outcome of the debate there is little doubt that large areas of the world are undernourished and some are constantly on the brink of famine and death. These societies present urgent problems for birth regulation and much-needed support while they raise their standard of living.

On a more personal level, more than one reason operates. Slater and Woodside quote eighteen reasons given for restricting the size of family which are reproduced below in the order of frequency of mention:

Money
Housing
Educational opportunities for children
Insecurity
War, separation, fear of bombs
Wife's health
Severe confinements in past
Hardship in own childhood
Age
Husband wants wife to be free
Wife does not want to be tied
Husband's health
Marital discord
Worry, responsibility, etc.
Husband does not want wife to suffer
Wife fears pregnancy or childbirth
No more wanted
Large family means hardship

Commenting on this list the authors state:

Some gave no reason and others several. As will be seen, the dominant theme is one connected, in one way or another, with material standards and the economic factor. The motivations that come under this heading are not entirely selfish, as one might suppose. That there are monetary reasons for restriction implies that the parents are moved not by a desire for wealth, but by a need to keep up with the rising standards in their own social class. The needs of the prospective child are rated much higher than they used to be. The propaganda for child care, health and nutrition has had its effect. There is a much more generally felt wish to give the child the other advantages that prudence can obtain – better education, apprenticeship or training. Even in such personal desires as for a home of their own with a garden, the parents are often thinking of the benefit that their one or two children will obtain from these amenities. The parents remember their own childhood and are determined to do better than their own parents did for them. 'Better a few good than a lot poor' reflects the fact that a higher evaluation of children carries with it an increased emphasis on the welfare of the children themselves.[61]

These medical and social reasons provide the background against which birth control operates but within this wide framework what specific role does birth control play in the marriages with which this book is particularly concerned?

There can be little doubt that the timing of the first baby and the size of the family is of particular importance to the couple whose marriage is vulnerable. Here the restricted resources of the spouses can be seriously dissipated by the demands of the child, converting a relationship which is just viable into one that is non-viable. Slater and Woodside point out that the material reasons put forward for restricting the size of the family are indications of the desire on the part of the parents to give their children all the benefits which they can afford in a society with rising standards. However, before these material advantages can be enjoyed, the parents must be in a position to sustain a minimum effective emotional relationship with their children. Prior even to this, they need to have achieved a minimum stability in their own husband-wife relationship.

Mr and Mrs M. had been married for about eighteen months and were both Irish and in their early twenties. They came to seek urgent help from the Catholic Marriage Advisory Council because she had become pregnant. There was a note of desperation in her urgent and defiant request that 'something should be done about it'. This 'something' clearly did not involve abortion for her but she was adamant that a baby would ruin their marriage. A psychological evaluation amply confirmed this. Her husband had suffered much physical illness and was also psychiatrically disturbed with a history of threatened and attempted suicide. She was the more stable of the two but was also a very anxious person, brought up in an unhappy home. She declared that they lived for one another, which was the only way of keeping going. A child would ruin their precarious survival. Counselling was attempted but made little progress because of the enormous threat that the coming child presented to the precarious stability she had achieved with her husband. She was only comforted when adoption arrangements were set in motion.

An inadequate and hasty judgement about this couple could suggest they were selfish. If anxiety and insecurity are prominent features in the personality of a couple, particularly that of the wife, the pregnancy and the child are no longer joyful expectations but dire threats to personal survival. This threat can be mitigated by adequate birth control which allows time for the necessary emotional maturation to handle the extra burdens that a child imposes.

Anxiety is also a severe detractor from adequate sexual performance, particularly for the male, and from satisfaction for the wife. Here birth control may minimize the apprehension about a pregnancy sufficiently to allow a much better performance and enjoyment. Birth control, however, is not a universal panacea for psychological difficulties and may fail to achieve the desired result as shown by the following example.

B.K., twenty-one, fourteen months ago married, is dissatisfied with his sexual relationship. His wife is 'a bit afraid', he doesn't quite know why. She has attended a birth control clinic, where she has learnt how to use a cap, and he also uses a condom, so that there should be no danger of an unwanted pregnancy. His wife has always had a silly fear that she would die in childbirth, though he says he has 'laughed her out of it'. A further trouble is that she never gets any satisfaction. He knows he is too quick and tries to hold back, but it makes him 'all jumpy'. They have read a marriage manual but, while they find it useful, it did not solve this problem. Mrs K., a tense, inhibited and hypochondriacal girl of twenty-two, says she has never yet experienced orgasm. She wonders if anything is wrong with her because she never 'gets worked up' or the 'mood doesn't last'. It may be the stories she heard at school about sex and childbirth have put her off. ... To be on the safe side they use cap, chemical and condom at each act of intercourse.[62]

This couple quoted by Slater and Woodside illustrates more than one problem. If they had not been using contraceptives, much of the blame for the wife's feelings would have been attached to the husband for his lack of adequate concern. A great deal of marital disharmony arises in precisely these conditions when the husband's sexual activity is interpreted so that he appears to be acting as a callous aggressor. But in fact the roots of the problem exist already in one or both of the partners; covert difficulties become overt but are certainly not 'caused' by either partner. Effective and mutually acceptable birth control can assist in not aggravating underlying problems, but it cannot cure serious psychological difficulties any more than its absence can cause them. Opponents of birth control have also claimed that its use *causes* marital disharmony. A superficial examination of the above couple may lead to precisely this opinion and a good case can be made in the presence of such a severe physical distortion of the sexual act that this is bound to have adverse repercussions on the couple. This is to ignore the psychological difficulties that exist in the couple prior to the use of birth control and the danger that without birth control the anxiety and insecurity will reach such proportions as to make sexual relations impossible, or, if at all possible, will involve endless mutual recriminations.

Moving from the initial phase of the marriage prior to the arrival of children, to a later phase, Hare and Shaw found that for mothers, and to a lesser extent fathers, rates for physical and mental ill-health increased with family size, a critical point being reached with four children and more.[63] Others have not confirmed their findings and there is room for further research here by relating the size of the family to the more detailed personality features of the parents. There can be little doubt however that the findings of Hare and Shaw are confirmed in individual families seen in clinical work, where the capacity of the parents, particularly that of the mother, has been exceeded with manifestations of physical and psychological ill-health. These are precisely the conditions where effective birth regulation is vital. Unfortunately, it is in these very circumstances that fatigue, apathy and a feeling of helplessness on the part of the wife set up a vicious circle in which less and less care is given to effective birth control. The inevitable pregnancy which follows creates a crisis which appears insoluble except through abortion. The rational answer here is to assume that it is the husband's responsibility to ensure that a further pregnancy is avoided. Only too frequently, however, the husband of such a partnership is found to be psychologically incapable of controlling either his sexual urge or of ensuring that effective birth regulation is practised. Impulsive sexual activity, particularly in the presence of alcoholic inebriation highlights a woman's vulnerability and the absolute necessity in these circumstances to put into the hands of the wife effective means of birth control, provided she in turn is prepared to and is capable of using them.

Failure to use birth control is not confined to the aggressive drunken husbands nor to the inept, worn-out wives. There are more subtle reasons, conscious and deliberate or unconscious. Pregnancy is one way of curtailing the wife's freedom and independence.

Mr and Mrs R. had been married for eighteen months. He was thirty, she twenty-six. He was a chef and she worked as a cashier in the restaurant where he worked. She was an extrovert, friendly and outgoing. Prior to her marriage she went dancing frequently and was interested in amateur dramatics. Her husband was exactly the opposite. He disliked these social activities and preferred to stay at home. He remonstrated with his wife about this and later accused her of infidelity, which was strenuously denied. *Coitus interruptus* was practised and it was agreed to postpone conception until enough money had been saved for the necessary deposit on a house. The wife became unexpectedly pregnant and this was explained away as an 'accident'. But events proved it to be otherwise. Shortly after the birth of the child the husband had a nervous breakdown and was admitted to hospital. During his illness he admitted that he had deliberately made his wife pregnant as he could no longer tolerate his feelings of jealousy and the fear that he would lose her.

Here the predominant reason was jealousy, frequently associated with feelings of insecurity which were in fact very prominent in this man.

Inferiority feelings in the woman may bring about an urgent clamouring *for a pregnancy*, which can be one of the most reassuring experiences to overcome such fears. Mrs C. freely admitted that she stopped using her cap. Her husband was against this third child:

'He loves it now of course but he was dead set against it. For myself I am still terrified of having children, the actual labour haunts me for weeks in advance although every one of them was simple and easy. But the thrill of carrying is terrific. Nothing makes me feel more like a woman than when I am pregnant. It is the one thing that nobody can do for me and my husband seems to be able to do just about everything else.'

Contraceptive failure has thus to be carefully assessed in individual cases for it may represent much more than method failure. In these instances only the most careful appraisal of the marital relationship will be able to reveal the real motives.

Society is gradually reaching the position of appreciating that the primary purpose of sexual intercourse is a union of love between the spouses, which becomes fruitful on specific occasions when the partners are ready to create a new life and bestow upon it unconditionally the love it needs. To achieve this, effective and safe birth control is essential for all, but particularly for those whose relationship is precarious. Unfortunately those who need birth control most find it most difficult to practise it successfully. Research workers [43] point out the need for high and sustained motivation and co-operation between the partners as vital pre-requisites for successful contraception and these are precisely the very qualities least available in unstable marriages. Marriage counselling can in these circumstances reinforce the wife's motivation and ensure as far as it is possible that conception will not take place until the future of the marriage is decided. Such advice needs to be ably supported by a service which goes to the home and assists couples who are incapable of organizing effective contraception for themselves.

THIRTEEN

PSYCHIATRIC ILLNESS AND THE ROLE OF THE PSYCHIATRIST

IN the course of their work psychiatrists encounter a great deal of marital disharmony and breakdown. This frequently presents a problem. Only too often the public still associates psychiatric disturbance with 'madness' or the loss of control over their mental faculties with all the fear and anxiety this state conjures up for them. Psychiatric intervention has to overcome this fear, but having done this the work of the psychiatrist will be delineated by the contribution of different psychiatric states towards marital disturbance.

The classification of psychiatric illness is still a matter for discussion and controversy but a currently acceptable one would include five main categories. These are the organic psychoses, functional psychoses, neuroses, personality disorders and mental subnormality. What contribution do these categories make to marital pathology?

Almost every psychiatrist would agree that in order of frequency the personality disorders would come first, followed by the neuroses, with the psychoses and mental defect, briefly mentioned in chapter four, trailing well behind. These last two categories include manifestations of mental illness such as intellectual defects, delusions, and hallucinations which are the established symptoms of severe psychiatric illness. The clinical rarity of these serious disorders as direct agents for marital breakdown is corroborated by the evidence presented in the statistics of the Registrar General shown in table 2. Reference to this table indicates clearly the very low incidence of unsound mind, less than half per cent as a cause for dissolution of marriage.[10]

A more detailed analysis regarding the type of psychological disorder associated with marital breakdown has been made by Blacker[51] who studied 8,000 patients admitted between 1952 and 1954 to a psychiatric post-graduate hospital who had been

Table 2

	Total	Husband	Wife	Both
Total dissolutions and annulments	32,052	13,806	18,099	147
Annulments	647	329	314	4
Dissolutions on all grounds	31,405	13,477	17,785	143
Adultery		8,253	7,618	
Cruelty		232	4,430	
Desertion		4,359	4,489	
Any two or all three of adultery, cruelty, desertion		558	1,147	
Unsound mind		57	35	
Presumed Dead		18	27	
Others			39	

married at some time. Amongst these 8,000 patients there were 824 broken marriages, an incidence of just over ten per cent and, therefore, approximating very closely to the overall incidence found in England and Wales, ranging between eight and fourteen per cent of all marriages. The distribution of the main categories of disturbance varied a great deal. The disorders of personality contributed three times as much to the broken marriages as the psychoses did. Naturally, in a hospital responsible for treating the psychologically ill, psychoses will be much in evidence even though, except for schizophrenia, they are not a prominent cause of breakdown. In a Marriage Council not concerned specifically with psychiatric disturbances, a more representative sample of difficulties is met with. The evidence here is even stronger that the vast majority of marriages which run into serious conflict do so in the presence of marked personality disturbances.[64]

The view that marital breakdown is essentially the consequence of personality disorder needs further confirmatory evidence from epidemiological studies in hospitals, marriage councils, the probation service, the courts and random samples of the community. If all these studies confirm the general trend that is emerging, then this clearly will need a detailed understanding by society itself, the courts, all those concerned with marriage and the couples themselves.

This understanding can only be reached slowly and reluctantly. The concrete experience of housing, financial, and sexual difficulties or family interference makes an immediate impact on the couple, who naturally feel they need not look any further for the 'cause' of their marital tension. Furthermore, society reinforces this judgement by emphasizing these very same explanations whenever the opportunity arises. The personality of each individual is the end product of a list of constitutional and environmental factors. Some of the traits are conscious and some unconscious. Not only is it not possible to reach the unconscious ones but the penetrating and exhausting examination required to reach an adequate insight of one's self is not a task which recommends itself. This is specially so if 'insight' means facing some painful or socially unacceptable trait which, in any case, is not easily removable even after the discovery has been made.

There is thus a very good reason, individually and collectively as a society, to emphasize those elements which place the responsibility outside oneself and which hold out a hope for change or improvement through alteration of the environment or another person. Nevertheless, if society is going to come to grips with the nature of marital pathology, the primacy of the emotional interpersonal conflict has to be recognized and dealt with.

It is because the emotional relationships of marriage are so important that the contributions of the dynamic schools of personality have been prominent throughout this book. These schools do not distinctly differentiate personality disorders from the neuroses and thus contribute to the difficulty in classification already mentioned. The Freudians, for example, see all neuroses as stemming from inadequately resolved libidinal conflicts, giving rise to anxiety which in turn is allayed by neurotic defence mechanisms. Adler emphasized the significance of inferiority feelings and saw in neuroses various compensatory patterns. The Neo-Freudians took as their stand the child's need for security, love and affection and its efforts to overcome the sense of helplessness and dependence of its early years. Common to all these views is the importance of early experiences in childhood when basic patterns of relationships are established *interpersonally*, primarily between child and parent. These are repeatable in future intimate relationships, and are hence of particular significance in understanding marital pathology.

But as mentioned already, personality is also determined by the innate characteristics of the person and their genetic make-up. The schools of psychology concerned with these aspects have paid special attention to the physiological basis of the constitution, particularly to those traits involving emotional lability such as excitability, tension and anxiety. Neuroses are now classified, not on a preconceived dynamic plan of interpersonal disturbance but on the presence and intensity of symptoms in which anxiety is prominent.

NEUROSES

It is the purpose of this chapter to describe only those details of the main psychiatric illnesses which are clearly relevant to marital pathology. Neuroses consist of four principal conditions namely anxiety neuroses, phobias, obsessional neurosis and hysteria. Phobias are characterized by attacks of unwarranted fear in the presence of certain objects or situations which would normally be considered harmless. In obsessional neurosis the patient experiences a repetition of thoughts and feelings or carries out actions compulsively against an inner feeling of resistance which by itself is incapable of ending the compulsive behaviour. The term 'hysteria' is used widely in two different ways, most commonly as a description of hysterical behaviour usually involving immature and emotionally exaggerated actions, and the neurosis itself, which involves loss of function of a mental or physical nature without an underlying organic lesion. All these conditions, with the exception of the hysterical personality, may be found from time to time in association with marital pathology but there is no evidence of any special connexion between them.

Since the anxious personality plays such an important part in marital work, anxiety neurosis will, however, be considered in some detail.

Anxiety is a rather loosely used term indicating a feeling of apprehension, uneasiness or fear which may or may not be accompanied, depending on intensity, by physiological manifestations such as palpitations, sweating, blushing, trembling, dry mouth, nausea or even vomiting. Some of these symptoms are experienced universally before testing situations such as examinations or in times of danger. Excessive anxiety is also present frequently in a variety of so-called psychosomatic illnesses. Some skin disorders and gastro-intestinal pathology such as peptic ulceration, asthma and migraine have earned a particular reputation for being associated with tense, anxious people. In fact these conditions have a multiple aetiology but there is little doubt that the presence of undue anxiety aggravates them. This is, of course, of particular importance in marital pathology when cruelty is being advanced as a cause for divorce since these conditions are aggravated by the mounting tension and the accused spouse is held solely responsible and blamed for 'causing' them.

Anxiety is frequently associated with people suffering from the personality difficulties mentioned in Chapters 6, 7, 8, 9, 10 and 11, in particular when the person lives with feelings of marked inadequacy and inferiority. Such persons constantly expect their limitations to be exposed, criticized, and ridiculed. Consciously and unconsciously they live with the fear of being found wanting. Any situation which has the quality of being a trial, however mild in character, becomes an occasion of exaggerated fear of expecting to be found useless, judged and condemned. The behaviour of others is interpreted through these fearsome expectations. Naturally such an image of one's self demands constant watch to conceal the real or imaginary deficiencies and much anxiety is involved in this work of protection. It also generates a lot of resentment and hostility for the behaviour of others which is considered to be hurtful, threatening, critical and unsympathetic.

But anxiety need not be concerned with these personal feelings and it is found in other persons who feel otherwise reasonably content and secure in their personality. Any situation which does not go according to plan, any unexpected events and, in general, any occasions which would not be a source of stress to others become moments of the most acute distress for them. Expectation of disaster round the corner is a living reality for them: the slight delay of the arrival of a member of the family denotes a fatal or, if not fatal, at least a terrible accident. Spouses and children are often imagined to be at death's door and the imagination runs wild with fears and terrors. In a proportion of both groups the manifestations of the anxiety are internal, creating an acute sense of discomfort, tension and agitation. In others the symptoms are expressed in more recognizable physical forms.

Anxiety is a very common symptom, perhaps the commonest that doctors are called upon to deal with. By itself it presents no specific threat to marriage. But when it is present in one or both spouses who are also experiencing relationship problems, then it adds a specific burden which can aggravate the situation gravely. Hence there is a very real need to use every available pharmacological agent to minimize the symptoms and thus enable the partners to examine the emotional aspects of the relationship. In marital pathology more than anywhere else it is absolutely necessary to go beyond the mere suppression of symptoms to their source. If their origin is an unsatisfactory relationship, this has to be identified and rectified as far as is possible. Drugs alone do not mend human relationships although they can frequently assist by relieving the anxiety and tension sufficiently to make the wider work of reconciliation possible.

PSYCHOSES

After personality disorder and the neuroses, the psychoses make a small contribution to marital breakdown. Unlike the first two these conditions are associated with severe mental symptoms in which delusions, hallucinations and marked impairment of mental function feature prominently. Organic psychoses can be dismissed briefly as the overwhelming number of those affected belong to the senile, involutional phase of the life circle in which marital disharmony is not prominent. On rare occasions brain damage is sustained in younger people as the result of injury, infection, neoplasm or even early senile changes. When death does not supervene rapidly, a spouse is left with a husband or wife who is either a semi-permanent invalid functioning at a much lower level of efficiency than before or who has to be taken care of permanently in a mental hospital. The healthy spouse has to suffer the deprivation of emotional and sexual support as well as carrying the emotional and economical burden of sustaining the family. In these rare and tragic situations conscience, stability and the prior quality of the marriage will govern the behaviour of the unaffected spouse.

Of the functional psychoses, schizophrenia is the most important for our subject. It has its onset in the second, third and fourth decade and is characterized by disturbances in thinking, the emotions and in behaviour, the latter being affected by the presence of delusions and hallucinations which are common and prominent manifestations.

In a very common variant, known as paranoid schizophrenia, the patient finds himself at the mercy of hostile and persecutory forces, often feeling the victim of a plot against him. In this deluded state the spouse may become the hostile figure and part of the alleged conspiracy. Feelings of intense, inexplicable and unshakable jealousy may be part of this condition, although jealousy often belongs to a variant of personality disturbance in which extreme personal insecurity fosters continuous doubts about the trustworthiness of the intimate figures surrounding the person. In paranoid schizophrenia the spouse may receive abuse and, on rare occasions, aggression and violence which can take an extreme form; sometimes the spouse is accused of infidelity, perhaps also of the most foul sexual transgressions. Auditory hallucinations are a common manifestation of this condition and may command the patient to inflict some sort of personal injury but more often they involve an unpleasant and unceasing barrage of accusations. With the recent major advances in the treatment of psychoses, these acute manifestations can often be brought quickly under control and the delusions recede. Despite these advances and a greater ability to keep such patients in the community in a functioning capacity, there is a certain amount of deterioration in the personality of some which shows itself in gradual withdrawal, inactivity, reduction in the number of personal relationships and a blunting of emotions and feelings.

These defects in the personality may be expected to have an adverse effect on the marriage rate for schizophrenics, and such is indeed the case. Several studies have confirmed the finding that the marriage rate among schizophrenics is lower and, in some studies, much lower than a comparable group in the population. The celibacy rate in a recent study was calculated to be fifty per cent above that of the general population.

The ability of the marriage to survive this strain will depend entirely on the resources of the family and particularly on the make-up of the spouse who has to shoulder the extra responsibility. The schizophrenic's diminished ability to cope with intense emotional demands, as a result of affective blunting, has deleterious consequences in the family setting. There is evidence indicating that the schizophrenic's chances of remaining well are increased by returning to a home in which the emotional demands placed on him will be low and within his capacity to handle. The dangers to marriage are obvious and the schizophrenic has not only a high celibacy but a high marriage breakdown rate. This is shown most markedly when the patient has to stay for long periods in hospital. In a study carried out entirely on schizophrenics, comprising 399 men and women followed up for five years, forty-four per cent of the ever married men and twenty-seven per cent of the women had separated or divorced.[65] The significance of this finding is not only the very high incidence of breakdown but the need to examine very carefully the population from which the figures are derived. Blacker's figures mentioned above represent the findings in a psychiatric hospital which does not cater for long-term patients and is mainly concerned with first illnesses. A percentage of these first breakdowns have recurrences which need further and continuous hospitalization and out of this group, the chronic schizophrenics, emerges this high incidence of breakdown which undoubtedly contributes to the bulk of the Registrar General's numbers under the unsound mind category.

There is a small group, which in all probability belongs to the general group of schizophrenics, in whom a paranoid disturbance of a marked degree emerges in the fifth, sixth and seventh decades. Here, after many years of happy marriage, perhaps twenty or thirty, one or the other spouse will begin to accuse the partner of marked infidelity. The accusations are persistent and supported by a mass of circumstantial evidence. Personal clothing will be found marked with lipstick, or powder, 'seminal' stains discovered and offered as 'proof'; telephone calls are assumed to be messages from the lover and visits outside the home will be interpreted as illicit rendezvous with the unknown seducer. Explanations, refutations, pleadings of innocence will all be to no avail as, in fact, this is a delusional illness not open to correction by reasonable explanation. Here a great deal of help can be given to the tormented partner. In some cases the intensity of the persecution may be alleviated by drugs, provided the patient is willing to take them, a matter of considerable difficulty as he will not entertain any suggestion that there is anything wrong with him. The survival of such a marriage will once again depend on the ability of the spouse to tolerate this situation. The duration of the relationship and the usually excellent relationship beforehand tend to help these marriages to survive.

The other common psychotic illnesses are called affective illnesses. These are characterized by specific changes in the mood of the person. Most people experience fleeting periods in which their mood is above or below its normal acceptable level. When these periods become protracted and the mood change is intense, depression or mania sets in.

Depression is characterized by a kind of overwhelming misery which leaves the patient deprived of any sense of well-being, with no hope for the future, no desire to live, eat or survive. He feels abandoned by everyone and postulates a large number of crimes and other self-accusatory actions which are responsible for his state. These illnesses are now open to effective treatment and, since they are limited in duration, do not cause the strain that schizophrenic ones do. In fact, acute illness of this sort does not present any major contribution to marital breakdown.

Depression, however, can have different forms of severity and in the absence of the above acute manifestations people may suffer sufficient depression to curtail severely their energy and effectiveness without reaching the extremes outlined above. These less severe cases, which are frequently associated with personality difficulties, present a much more serious menace for a marriage that may be already labouring under relational strain. Frequently, the depression is a response to the difficult situation at home, while it itself aggravates the problem by the deterioration of the effective functioning capacity of the person.

The housewife, who is chronically dispirited and fatigued, finds herself unable to cope with her work. Her husband may be accused of not helping or of expecting too much of her. This may be true but even when he does help, although this relieves the situation somewhat, it cannot bring about an inner sense of well-being. The despondency and frustration continue until the next crisis is reached when the husband will be blamed afresh and there will come the day when he is not prepared to take any more criticism. Since depression of any form tends to disorganize the major physiological functions, including the sexual ones, reduced desire deprives the wife of another source of personal significance to her, adding a load of guilt feelings and leaving her husband increasingly isolated and unable to reach her. Isolation does not only result from the withdrawal of the hurt and angry partner. It is a marked characteristic of depression itself, contributing to the person's unwillingness to face social contacts, leading to withdrawal and a sense of helplessness in coping with even the simplest demands. Unless this withdrawal is understood by the spouse as part of the depressive temperament, its exhibition is taken as further 'proof' of the ill-intent of the sufferer.

Another aspect of depression is its cyclical character, descending upon a person for a few days or weeks and then lifting again or even drifting to mild euphoria. Such recurrent cycles, unless clearly recognized, have a profound impact on relationships and work. In a good phase closeness is achieved, plans are made, hopes raised and activity pursued with enthusiasm. As the depression descends, there is a marked withdrawal for which some irrelevant incident will be blamed. The fervour of the activity will diminish and even best-laid plans will not be put into operation. These variations in mood are the simple explanation for one of the commonest accusations made by spouses against each other, namely that they are unreliable. Since they are incomprehensible, both to the sufferer and to the onlookers, alternative explanations of social and moral inadequacy are sought. These episodes of depression are of the greatest importance in marriage because if the sufferer is already laden with feelings of inferiority and of guilt, these periods of recurrent inactivity, even if they are not used by the spouse as weapons of attack – accusations of laziness, selfishness, etc. – are interpreted as further evidence of personal inadequacy. A mild to moderate depression, frequently accompanied by anxiety symptoms, which goes on unchecked for long periods, is utterly demoralizing for both partners and hence the intervention of appropriate treatment is essential.

A depressive or schizophrenic illness may appear following the birth of a child. The incidence of these severe post-puerperal illnesses has been variously calculated to be one in 400–1,200 deliveries. They require hospitalization and all the active treatment that is currently available. The impact of these severe illnesses in the marriages were followed up in eighty-one cases studied at Shenley Hospital and fourteen were found to end in separation or divorce, an incidence of seventeen per cent, which is slightly higher than that for the average population.[66]

In addition to these psychotic illnesses there is frequently a very brief phase of maternity blues in which a certain amount of depression and tearfulness may be present. This lowering of morale and reduction of energy clears up in most cases but not in all.

There remains another group of puerperal problems, which are intimately associated with the above depressive illnesses, but which are not usually recognized as illnesses, either by the doctor or by the patient herself. After a prolonged period, which in one case was as long as nine years, they finally arrive at a marriage council. The immediate problem is the deteriorating relationship between husband and wife with the contemplation of a separation or divorce. The story is not usually distinguishable from the familiar pattern of accusations and counter-accusations until, either accidentally or through specific questioning, one or other spouse admits that the problem started with the birth of the last child.

What emerges then is a stereotyped tale. Following the birth of the child, the mother feels tired and lacks her usual energy. She becomes irritable and snappy with the other members of the family. This sort of behaviour may have been usual for her previously, in which case it becomes markedly more severe or unusual and out of keeping with her character. These symptoms are explained away by the arrival of the new child with the increased load it imposes on the mother. In addition to the marked fatigue and irritability, there is a diminution of sexual desire varying from a total loss and avoidance of all sexual relations to a reluctant and non-enjoyable resumption for the sake of the husband. Everyone expects the situation to improve and in the interval the husband and the relatives give a helping hand. But the situation does not change and after a few months benevolent patience gives way to muted criticism and then to open grumbling by the husband who is no longer able to recognize his wife. She is criticized on the grounds that she is not really trying and in no time at all the words 'selfish', 'irresponsible', and 'lazy' are being flung about. The wife is trying desperately all the time to emerge from this wretched state and cannot. After a while the marriage begins to suffer and the situation gradually deteriorates to the point where a break-up is contemplated. If the correct diagnosis of a prolonged and persistent post-puerperal syndrome is made and appropriate treatment instituted, these marriages can benefit tremendously. One couple with the above problems were able within a matter of weeks to go to the theatre after nine years of being confined to the house.

This concluding section will deal briefly with the role of the psychiatrist in marital disorder. Every psychiatrist has an important part to play in the diagnosis and treatment of the area acknowledged by everyone to be his sole domain, namely the psychoses. As already noted, however, this is a minute contribution to the total pathology of marital breakdown.

The majority of severe marital problems will be accounted for by personality disorder, accentuated by the presence of anxiety in its various forms. Thus marital disorder highlights a waning but still recognizable tension within psychiatry itself between psychiatrists whose main interest lies broadly in the 'organic' field involving the psychoses and an interpretation of neuroses on non-dynamic lines, and those who favour the 'dynamic' approach, mainly analysts, psychotherapists and general psychiatrists with a special interest in the dynamic approach.

This is, of course, confusing for a society which reasonably enough expects all psychiatrists to be capable of giving a uniform evaluation of these problems. Unfortunately this is not the case and it accounts for the occasional apparently contradictory reports given on the same marriage.

At the present moment the general training of all psychiatrists requires that they should elicit information about the stability of the patient's marriage whenever possible since marital tension is such an important contributing factor to symptomatology. Beyond this, however, each psychiatrist will be left with a variable knowledge of, interest in, or concern for the mechanisms of marital pathology. This is an unsatisfactory situation and the basic training of the future should include specific reference to these problems.

As the psychological and sociological knowledge on this subject grows psychiatrists familiar with it will be better equipped to tackle this all-too-familiar problem. At present, after commencing with a pharmacological approach to alleviate anxiety and mood disturbance, they make a comprehensive evaluation of the emotional disturbance based on an eclectic dynamic approach. Neither the rigidity of orthodox Freudian psychology nor that of certain organic psychiatrists has anything useful to contribute in the management of these problems.

When the necessary motivation is present what is required is a careful appraisal of the affectionate and instinctual needs and tensions of the couple, bearing in mind the situation of the whole family. With the assistance of the full therapeutic team of doctors, nurses, psychiatric social worker and psychologist, treatment should aim at the restoration of an effective communication between spouses which allows sufficient resolution of conflicts and fulfilment of mutual needs to allow the marriage to proceed on its own momentum.

Marital work is undoubtedly time-consuming and clearly far too many psychiatric teams are overwhelmed with routine work to attempt anything additional. The allocation of priorities remains one of the challenging tasks for every doctor, not least the psychiatrist, confronted as he is by an ever-widening professional involvement. The needs of the family make compelling demands and the likelihood of their receiving a higher priority will depend on the competence of the basic psychiatric training in this subject. Psychiatrists and doctors in general would be more willing to tackle marital problems if they were more conversant with the nature of the pathology and felt more optimistic about the outcome of intervention.

It is unlikely that there will be enough specialists in this field in the near future to meet all the needs of the community. Hence psychiatrists can play a particularly useful role in assisting the training of marriage counsellors and all those who are involved in marital reconciliation.

FOURTEEN

OUTCOME

THE impact of marital breakdown on the family is difficult to assess and so far few studies which have attempted to do this in detail exist. In any case, it would be difficult to encompass the range and intensity of suffering which afflicts both partners and the children. Personal or second-hand experience in the privacy of the consulting room reveals the depth of misery which at times tests human endurance beyond its capacity. Autobiographies and narratives are better equipped to portray the individual conflicts and complexities of the situation. Only a brief description will be given here of the little that is known and has been studied objectively. The spouses and the children will be considered separately.

Prior to the irrevocable decision to separate or divorce there is a period of mounting tension characterized by quarrels and physical or psychological ill-health. Arguments may be frequent and the scene is set occasionally for one of those episodes of family violence which casualty departments, psychiatric units and police stations witness from time to time. These outbursts often occur in the evening or at night when the presence of excess alcohol diminishes control, fans hostility and propels the violence of pent-up feelings into action. Alternatively quarrels may be infrequent or absent and the mounting tension is expressed through physical symptoms. Insomnia, headaches, aches and pains in different parts of the body, fatigue and restlessness are common manifestations with which the family doctor is asked to help. In the presence of so much frustration and suffering, the inevitable depression that accompanies them may reach such proportions that desperate action follows. There are those who feel that the end of the marriage spells the end of their personal survival. Suicides and attempted suicides at this critical moment are not uncommon. The cry one often hears: 'I don't want to live now that he (or she) has gone, there is nothing to live for' is one that can prove temporarily unanswerable. Unlike the loss by death, with its period of mourning and recovery, this loss is accentuated by personal responsibility and guilt from which it is difficult to escape.

The continuous lack of affection, coupled with the gradual withdrawal and mutual alienation, creates the right conditions for eliciting and responding to the sympathy and support of others. Since there are many people in similar situations, they provide a constant pool of married and unmarried who will turn to one another to provide the love and affection missing at home. Thus the other man or woman who arrives on the scene will frequently be not the cause of the marital breakdown but the product of the prevailing situation.

Even if the third and fourth parties are not actually present at or about the time of the dissolution, evidence both from the United Kingdom and the U.S.A. indicates that between seventy to eighty per cent of divorcees remarry.[67, 68] The success of these remarriages has been noticed by many authorities who have drawn conflicting conclusions. There can be no doubt that second marriages can be most successful but what is the chance of this compared with the success and stability of first marriages? Information on this question is scarce and a good deal more research is required. Monahan has reported a detailed study in the State of Iowa in the United States.[69] In the years 1953–55 there were 70,901 marriages with 15,502 divorces. The divorce rate per hundred marriages contracted was calculated from selected types of marital breakdown and the results are shown in Table 3.

The author points to the stability of the widowed but remarks that 'Our divorce rate is being compounded by the repetitiousness of divorce among a divorce-prone population group and there seems to exist in our American system a dual pattern of marriage, with "sequential polygamy" being the practice of a substantial minority of the population entirely within the law.'

These demographic results are confirmed in the findings of other cities in the United States and tally perfectly with the

Table 3

Ratio of divorces per hundred marriages of selected type of marital background in Iowa U.S.A. 1953–5.

Type of marital background	Ratio	Type of marital background	Ratio
Overall incidence	21·9	One divorced once, other twice or more	62·1
Both at first marriage	16·6	Both divorced twice or more	79·4
One first marriage, other divorced once	36·8	Both widowed once	9·9
Both divorced once	34·9	One widowed once, other first marriage	16·1

view that the divorcee belongs to a group of vulnerable personalities. With the passage of time, some of these emerge from their difficulties sufficiently to be able to effect and maintain successful human relationships in a subsequent marriage, while others carry their basic difficulties within themselves and suffer a similar fate in subsequent encounters. Thus for some spouses there is the ultimate possibility of a dissolution and the prospect of happiness in a second attempt. Despite Samuel Johnson's warning that to marry a second time represents the triumph of hope over experience, a large majority do just this and achieve much more than Dr Johnson dared to believe. Unfortunately, marital breakdown involves more than two adults. The children of such marriages, who did not ask to become either witnesses or participants in some of the bitterest manifestations of human intolerance, antagonism and hatred, pay a heavy price. They are deprived, through no fault of their own, of their right to feel secure and loved by the authors of their life, and are frequently manipulated or pushed to take sides with one party. The much desired and needed positive image of both parents is distorted beyond recognition by the real or imaginary grievances of one of them, which the child cannot understand or evaluate. Their loyalty is torn beyond endurance when, in committing themselves to either parent, they have to identify themselves with one point of view at the expense of the other, only to discover many years later the dubiousness of their position and at times the complete falsity of the attitude which they were trapped into adopting, Alienated from one parent through the need to keep close to at least one source of love, they discover later the truc perspective of things without always having the opportunity or possibility of rectifying previous injustices. Witnesses of scenes of violence and anger in their early and impressionable years, their earliest memories are of parents hurting each other, incapable of trusting or showing mutual respect. The situation is even worse where the child becomes a shuttlecock between the parents, no longer a concern of their love but an object, a tool, to obtain what they cannot achieve by any other means. It is not surprising that in such circumstances children develop a host of physical and psychological manifestations. School work deteriorates and a variety of conduct and behaviour disorders emerge.

If the final parting is painful for the parents, even if inevitable and necessary, this last act of the human drama presents the child with an agonizing and, humanly speaking, impossible decision. The child's wishes may be taken into account, but frequently it is the mother who is given custody of the child and this very often is the best answer to a difficult situation. But a child needs both father and mother, and even the very best decision cannot replace the missing parent. This is the most painful moment for the child, who finds itself without one parent through no fault of its own, forced to make a choice between the parents and to make the best of a state which is not of its own making. The intensity of the suffering can be minimized a great deal by careful handling and management of the situation and a lot depends, of course, on the age of the child. Children who have reached a mature enough age to understand the situation without being utterly perplexed and mystified, and those who are too young to understand what is happening at all, suffer least at the actual point of separation, but the intermediate group experience in full the pangs of separation, of divided loyalties and loss. Once again they may experience a host of physical and psychological symptoms and both school work and behaviour may deteriorate. With skilful handling, however, in which personal vendettas, hostilities and anger are kept to the minimum by the spouses, the situation may be eased. And if an attempt is made to show the departing parent in the best possible light, with the minimum of criticism, the child may not suffer too much in what is frequently for him a confused muddle.

It may be that undue emphasis has been placed on the suffering of the child at the time of separation. Continuous marital disharmony, with the tensions and repeated quarrels, impinges just as sharply on the child. The effect on the child is very much in the forefront of the argument between those who advocate wider facilities for divorce and those who oppose any extension. The opponents of divorce argue that the child's welfare is imperilled by the dissolution of the family, while the advocates conclude that in the presence of persistent disharmony the child cannot escape danger and it is kinder to bring the marriage to an end. Instances in which both points of view can be defended are quoted, but all the evidence in the world is not a satisfactory alternative to adequate research and follow-up studies, which are extremely few.

Persistent maternal or paternal deprivation, but particularly the former, has been the subject of much psychiatric research. Bowlby's contribution has had a lasting influence in this field and his conclusion that there is a relationship between prolonged mother-child separation and serious personality disturbance is of the greatest importance. Bowlby's early conclusions, which are being further examined, widen the meaning of deprivation.[70] Some of the implications for marital breakdown were examined in chapter seven.

In an extensive and detailed investigation of the social outlook for children of divorcees, carried out in Malmo, the third largest city in Sweden, 606 families, in which the spouses were legally divorced in the period 1920–31, were followed up from the time of the divorce up to 1949. A third of the dissolved marriages were childless. Ultimately 1,464 children of the remaining families were traced and, of these, 1,333 persons, 676 men and 657 women, were studied in detail. Several social characteristics were examined and their incidence in the children of the divorced families was compared with that of the general population.[71]

The number of boys who had to be admitted for reform schooling was 6·6 per cent, which was four times as high as the risk for the general population at Malmo. The risk for girls – normally lower than boys – was only twice as high. More than twenty per cent of the men would have been convicted of a felony if they lived till they were fifty years of age as compared to 9·9 per cent of the male population. This doubled incidence is also present in women. By the age of forty, the cumulative risk of serious alcoholism was three times as high.

A close relationship has also been found between the broken home, and psychiatric illness and personality disorder. Particular attention has been given to suicidal attempts. Significant correlations have been found between suicidal behaviour later in life and parental loss in childhood, loss being defined as continuous absence for at least twelve months of one or both natural parents before the age of fifteen. Compared with non-suicidal patients, the suicidal patients had a significantly high incidence of parental loss, and such loss commonly involved both parents, occurred at a younger age and was more frequently due to irreversible causes such as parental death or divorce.[72] A further study by the same authors showed that a significantly greater proportion of those attempting suicide came from broken homes and had experienced recent disruption of a close relationship in the previous six months than from intact homes.[73] This is a very important finding, indicating the continuous and accumulative risks involved. As we have seen there is good evidence to suggest that people from broken homes have an above-average risk that their own marriage will suffer, with the likelihood of disturbed personal relationships.

One important feature in the outcome as far as the child is concerned, is the degree of *disorganization* that is brought about by the broken home situation and the subsequent *harmony* achieved between itself and its step-parents. Two studies have shed some light indirectly on this matter. In his studies of parental loss and suicidal attempts quoted above,

Greer[74] found that there was a significant relationship between diagnostic category and the subsequent childhood environment after parental loss. Thirty per cent of sociopaths (personality disorders) had spent at least one year in an orphanage as compared to only nine per cent of those suffering from neurotic illness. Since personality disorder carries a greater likelihood of unstable personal relationships, the future of such people is thus likely to be further influenced adversely by an unsatisfactory environment after the parental home has been disrupted.

A similar finding was also discovered accidentally in a Swedish study of delinquent boys, their parents and grandparents.[75] The author studied 305 delinquent boys and compared them with 500 boys attending child guidance cilinics and 222 non-delinquent normal ones. He found that forty-two per cent of the delinquent boys were sons of divorced parents as against only thirteen per cent of the non-delinquent boys. This carries a high statistical significance suggesting the adverse overall effect of divorce.

He investigated this finding further by comparing the later adjustment of the children in the non-delinquent group who came from divorced parents and the others from intact homes. To his great surprise he found *no* difference. 'The adjustment of children of divorced parents was no worse than that of other children.' What was it that contributed to delinquency in one set of circumstances and not in another? He examined how the families were reconstructed after the divorce.

Table 4 shows very clearly that what happens after the divorce distinguishes the delinquent boys from the non-delinquent ones. The lack of visiting by the boy's father, antagonism between boy and step-father and the absence of any stability are obvious negative elements, while good relationships between boy and step-father and regular contact between himself and father are advantageous. The author sums up his findings in this sentence: 'The psychological reconstruction phase following the divorce probably meant more than the acute conflict during the divorce proceedings.'

The age of the child at the time of the separation or divorce

Table 4

Relationship of boys and their parents

	Delinquent boys number	Non-delinquent boys number
1 Mother alone; divorced father meets boy		
a. regularly	2	5
b. sporadically	2	1
c. never	14	5
d. divorced father forces himself on son against mother's wishes	4	—
2 Mother remarried		
a. good contact between boy and step-father	2	12
b. antagonism between boy and step-father	7	1
3 Father alone; forbids boy to meet mother	3	4
4 Father remarried; antagonism between boy and step-mother	2	—
5 Parents living together although not remarried, boy living with them	2	1
6 Neither parents remarried; boy moves from one to the other; antagonism between parents	4	—
7 Boy permanently in children's home; neither of parents visits him	3	—
Total	45	29

may prove also to be important. In the study at Malmo the research revealed that the consequences for the children were consistently more serious the younger the child was at the time of the parent's divorce. This was most obvious for those under four, but persists in some of the findings of the four to nine age group, although there is an overall amelioration with each successive older age group. Greer confirms this tendency in his study of the factors associated with suicidal attempts. He finds that neurotic and sociopathic patients with attempted suicides differed from similar patients who had not attempted suicide in (*a*) having a higher incidence of parental loss, (*b*) experiencing such loss more commonly before the age of five and (*c*) being deprived more frequently of both parents.

These studies point the way for future research. The impact on the child needs to be investigated in terms of such factors as age and future environment, to which may be added the sex of the child, the personality of the parent, usually the mother, and that of the step-parent.

In the United States, studies carried out in the fifties have suggested that it is not divorce itself but the atmosphere in the home which is the damaging agent. In his book *Children of Divorce*, J. L. Despert, a psychiatrist, states 'It is not divorce, but the emotional situation in the home, with or without divorce, that is the determining factor in a child's adjustment. A child is very disturbed where the relationship between the parents is very disturbed.'[76] Goode, in discussing children of divorce, states that: 'In all likelihood, almost every serious researcher in American family behaviour has suggested that the effects of continued home conflict might be more serious for the children than the divorce itself.'[8]

Landis,[77] pursuing this view, studied 3,000 college students and divided the men and women into three categories: happy, unhappy, and unhappy divorced homes. Relationships with parents, self evaluations and dating histories were compared. On most variables tested there were few statistical differences between children from divorced and unhappy non-divorced marriages, except for boys where their present relationship with their father was currently more distant with the divorced father than with the unhappy non-divorced father and this applied to the girls as well, both *before* and after the age of fifteen. The fact that children usually go with the mother after divorce partially explains this finding. The author suggests that other variables should be investigated, such as the age of the child during the period of unhappiness, the ability of the parents to meet the needs of the children when the parents are faced with a crisis, whether the parents remarry, whether the marriage is a happy or an unhappy one, how much the child is used as a go-between during and after the divorce, and socio-economic differences.

There is still a great deal of work to be done to answer satisfactorily all the questions posed by divorce as far as the child is concerned but it is abundantly clear that the consequences depend on many factors besides the court's decision.

One question, perhaps more than any other, has held the attention of research workers. How does the marriage of the parents influence that of their child?

All major studies so far are in agreement that the parental marriage experience itself and the links between the parents and the children are of paramount importance for the next generation's marital relationship. It has been established fairly convincingly that marital success is associated with a correspondingly high level of happiness in the parents and the absence of divorce and separation in their marriages.[78, 79]

The pattern of divorce was studied in three generations in the United States amongst 1,977 unmarried students.[80] 674 men and 1,303 women were asked to give the marital status of their grandparents and parents. A close relationship was found between the marital status of the grandparents and the parents of the students. If neither set of grandparents had divorced or separated, then the ratio of divorce to marriage was 1 to 6·8, if one set of grandparents had divorced or separated the ratio fell to 1 to 4·8 and if both sets had divorced or separated the ratio became 1 to 2·6. These associations are of course only statistical ones and cannot predict the outcome of individual cases, a point that should always be remembered in assessing statistical results.

These findings, however, closely correspond with clinical experience and are supplemented by studies showing that marital happiness is intimately associated with a childhood in which relations with the parents were close, with adequate affection effectively exchanged, discipline firm but kind and an absence of cruelty and unnecessary physical punishment.[81] There is thus considerable evidence to suggest that the existence of marital disharmony in one generation diminishes the chances of success in the next.

FIFTEEN

PREVENTION

SINCE the stability of a community is intimately connected with the welfare of the individual family unit, society has a triple responsibility regarding marriage. It has to provide a legal structure that safeguards life-long stability while making it possible for men and women to start afresh when their previous attempt has not succeeded. It needs to ensure that its citizens are protected as far as is possible from contracting marriages whose survival is extremely hazardous. Finally, it must provide all possible help to assist marriages in difficulties. Prevention, reconciliation and an effective system for dissolution are society's three responsibilities. Understandably, far too much emphasis has been placed on the last item but all three are intimately linked and progress in one must herald advances in the other two.

The work of prevention is extremely complicated because the facts on which to act are few and there are possible dangers in infringing the liberty of individuals. The subject, however, lends itself to an educational programme which recognizes some of the known risks. Here sociologists and psychiatrists have slowly accumulated information which highlights certain dangers. Sociologists have been concerned particularly with *the age* of the partners at marriage and the presence of *premarital pregnancy*.

Marriages are taking place at an earlier age for both sexes. Pierce [2] has estimated on the basis of a representative sample of couples married in Britain in the fifties, that twenty per cent of the brides had been married before their twentieth birthday, rising to a figure of ninety-three per cent whose wedding had taken place before their twenty-fifth birthday. The Registrar General's statistics confirm this in a different way. At the beginning of the century, twenty out of every thousand bachelors under the age of twenty were married. In 1963 this figure had risen to seventy-nine. The figures for spinsters were a hundred and four and three hundred and five respectively.[10] These figures clearly indicate the reduction of marriage age here, and there is a similar trend in the United States. Does this matter? Does age at marriage influence its outcome? This is one question relating to marriage breakdown that has received the most unequivocal affirmative. Every major study in the last thirty years and all the official statistics have found that age at marriage is associated with success, with a critical cut-off point at about eighteen to nineteen. Marriages below this age run a

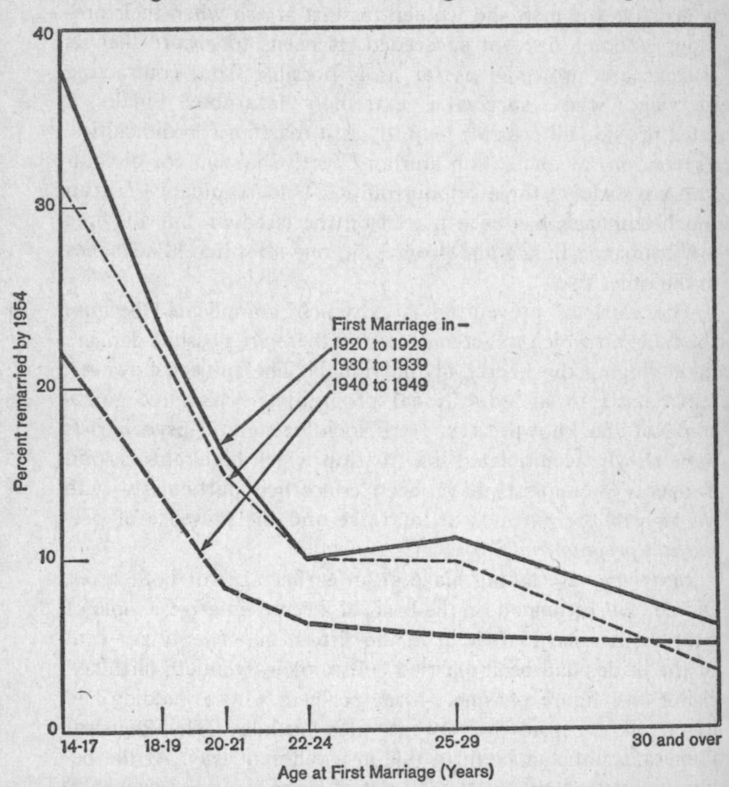

Figure 1. Graph showing percentage of women remarried by 1954, whose first marriages took place between 1920 and 1949

considerably higher risk of breaking down. This is illustrated in figure 1 from a census in the United States.[82]

The close relationship between early marriage and instability is clearly shown. The most impressive finding is the proportion of remarried women amongst those who first married below the age of eighteen, which is approximately three times as high as that for women who first married between the age of twenty-two to twenty-four. This relationship is present, independent of the year of the first marriage.

In Britain similar results were found by Rowntree[4] in a smaller national sample of 3,000 men and women aged between sixteen and fifty-nine, of whom 1,340 couples had married between 1930 and 1949.

Table 5 shows again in a very convincing manner that marriages in which the bride is nineteen or less are running a risk that is serious for all categories but particularly marked in the groups which are infertile or have premaritally conceived, another determinant discussed below.

There is no single explanation that can account for the marked vulnerability of these early marriages. Maturation is a process which involves the physical, emotional, social and spiritual aspects of human growth. These extremely early marriages involve men and women who have certainly attained sufficient growth to meet the requirements of sexual intercourse and reproduction. This physical development is plainly not enough to sustain the relationship through the trials of early marriage. So long as marriage was seen in the restricted sense of physical consummation, with or without procreation, the wider aspects of the union could be safely ignored. This is no longer a sufficiently meaningful concept and these so-called marriages break up because the wider significance of the relationship is not capable of developing.

What motivates a number of these marriages is the urgent need to get away from an unhappy situation and to find a substitute bastion of security. The forthcoming union is visualized as the deliverance from personal problems which appear insurmountable. The urgent need for closeness, companionship, support, security and/or the escape from an intolerable home

Table 5

Proportions of couples who had parted or had contemplated separation according to their fertility, the conception of their first child and the bride's age at marriage.

First child conceived	Bride's age	Number of couples	Proportion parting	Proportion contemplating separation
Infertile			%	%
	Up to 19	23	56·0	8·7
	20–24	72	19·5	1·4
	25 & over	133	4·5	—
	All ages	228	13·6	4·4
Fertile				
Before marriage	Up to 19	50	26·0	8·0
	20–24	89	6·8	9·0
	25 & over	37	8·1	
	All ages	176	12·2	6·8
After marriage	Up to 19	108	11·1	4·6
	20–24	496	7·2	2·2
	25 & over	330	3·0	3·9
	All ages	934	6·4	3·1
All couples		1338*	8·5	3·8

* Two cases in which the age of the bride at marriage was not recorded have been omitted from this table.

situation are amongst the commonest reasons offered. Unfortunately, the very circumstances that prompt such urgent action are exactly those which have least prepared the participants to overcome the difficulties which they have to face when the initial burst of enthusiasm wanes. The inexperience and emotional instability, which characterizes this situation, can be further aggravated by economic and housing difficulties. This is the period when earnings are small and initial expenses heavy. The combination of emotional immaturity and outstanding economic and housing difficulties often proves overwhelming.

Assisting young people in such a situation is difficult. Absolute prohibitions are neither constructive nor likely to reduce the size of the problem, particularly if the law allows the right of marriage at eighteen. The marriage appears to offer a magical solution to their problems and nothing else will do. Expert counselling is needed to promote a relationship between the counsellor and the young person which provides *outside* the genuine help and support that is sought *in* the marriage, thereby gaining time for adequate preparation.

Table 5 is not only concerned with the effect of age on marriages but the influence of fertility as well. Reference has already been made to the childless marriage in Chapter 12; here the significance of pre-marital pregnancy is considered. It will be seen that the percentage of couples who have parted or contemplated separation is distinctly higher in almost all ages in which there has been a pre-marital pregnancy. This is particularly marked in the under twenties. 12·2 per cent of all age groups had parted as compared to 26 per cent in the age group under nineteen complicated by a pre-marital pregnancy. Pre-marital pregnancy has an overall adverse effect which, when combined with an early marriage, produces the second highest incidence of complete breakdown. Rowntree's findings do not stand alone. In the United States the studies of Christensen and his colleagues have examined, over a span of some thirty years, the effect of pre-marital pregnancy on marriage, and have reached exactly the same result. Their findings cover a detailed analysis of marriages and divorces in two different states in the United States, Utah County, Utah, Tippecanoe County, Indiana, and in Copenhagen, Denmark. In one of his latest papers, Christensen sums up his findings thus: 'The conclusion that pre-marital pregnancy is more likely to be followed by divorce than post-marital pregnancy, and that early post-marital pregnancy is more likely to be followed by divorce than is delayed post-marital pregnancy seems almost inescapable'.[83] Christensen worked on the hypothesis that the most sexually permissive culture, in this case Denmark, would show the least negative effect and the most restrictive, that of the Mormon culture of Utah, the greatest. The results confirmed this but showed conclusively that, irrespective of such cultural relativism, pre-marital pregnancy has an adverse effect on marriage.

The reasons for these adverse results are not hard to find. Couples may marry because a child is on the way and not because they are suited to one another. If pregnancy follows sexual relations in which either, but usually the wife, was the unwilling but compliant partner, the marriage starts with a sense of grievance and a ready source of hostility, which will be unleashed repeatedly, whatever the nature of the underlying difficulties. Excessive guilt and anxiety are generated in pre-marital pregnancy through the feelings of moral transgression and by the judgement which the couple expect from others. Independent of these possible social censures, the couple start marriage with their attention diverted from one another towards the child and this is a deprivation which some cannot survive.

The implications of these findings are many and important. Pre-marital pregnancy is clearly a threat to the future of the marriage, particularly in the very young. The avoidance of pregnancy can be achieved by pre-nuptial continence or the use of effective contraception. The factors which influence either choice are complex and lie beyond the scope of this book. What is vital, however, is to avoid hasty marriages for religious or social reasons when a pregnancy occurs. Pre-marital pregnancy is not a good reason for marriage; marriage should not be undertaken unless the couple are ready and capable of undertaking it. Support for the unmarried mother, facilities to help her to keep the child, efficient and rapid adoption and counselling to meet both the young man's and girl's difficulties are essential, but so is education beforehand which points out the danger of pre-marital pregnancy.

To age and pre-marital pregnancy can be added the *engagement period* as the third factor studied extensively by sociologists and in this case also by psychiatrists. It might be expected that, if this preparatory phase meets with success, the prospects for the marriage itself are good and vice versa. This indeed has been found to be the case. Burgess and Wallin,[84] who carried out a most detailed examination of engagement success, followed up their subjects after some years of marriage and confirmed the prediction that success in this phase was followed by success later on. Indeed these authors claim that their engagement success score was found to be the best single instrument available before marriage for the prediction of marital success. The duration of acquaintance and engagement has been examined by many of the principal studies and the general conclusion that a short period of acquaintance and engagement is associated with a high incidence of marital unhappiness is confirmed by nearly every one. The actual time recorded as a minimum requirement differs from study to study, although there is some agreement indicating that at least nine months of engagement provides an average probability for success. Too much stress cannot be placed on actual figures but the general trend is of importance. Marriages following a casual and brief acquaintanceship, usually based on a physical infatuation without the opportunity to test the personal characteristics that will have to stand the stresses and strains of everyday life, are, if not doomed to failure, seriously handicapped from the very beginning.

Hasty marriages, for whatever reason, are risky propositions. In their more extreme forms they are connected with elopements and the Gretna Green type of ceremony. Studies of both have been carried out in the United States. In what is probably a unique collection and examination of elopements, Popenoe [85] found, in his 738 cases, a happy outcome was the result in only forty-eight per cent, which shows a very marked reduction from average expectations of about eighty per cent. The Gretna Green type of marriage is characterized by earlier age for legal contract and only a short waiting period, if any. In America, Elkton in Maryland, and Kahoka in Missouri had a nationwide publicity at one time for being the towns for the 'quick marriage'. Kephart and Strohm [86] examined the records of a sample of such Gretna Green marriages in Elkton, Maryland, and

Media, Pennsylvania, and found a significant increase in the frequency of divorce in these marriages.

Elopements and Gretna Green marriages are interesting rarities; the broken engagement, on the other hand, is not so rare, comprising some ten per cent of the 1,000 engaged couples which Burgess and Wallin investigated. These authors found that slight attachment shown by poor demonstration of affection, short acquaintance and engagement, marked separation indicated by short period spent together, parental opposition, cultural and social differences, religious and personality difficulties were the main factors associated with broken engagements. It is more than likely that some of these factors are not independent entities, but stem from a common cause. Here, as in the whole field of marriage studies, it is vital to go beyond the disturbed social manifestations to the basic reasons, which not infrequently will be found in the psychological make-up of the individuals. There is some confirmatory evidence for this, as far as the engagement is concerned, from psychiatric sources. From as long ago as 1888 mental disorders connected with marriage and engagements have been described in psychiatric literature. Recently Davies [87] described in detail the various manifestations of psychiatric illness in a group of men and women admitted to hospital in whom the precipitating factor was their engagement. They expressed doubts about its future and responded with anxiety and depression of sufficient severity to need medical attention. These patients were found to have a high incidence of neurotic and personality disturbances.

The broken engagement leading to a psychiatric breakdown is one form of response to the coming marriage. Hospital admission may not be necessary. The following account is given by a young woman of high intelligence who was trying to solve the difficulties of her engagement in a marriage council. The conflict between reason and the emotions is rarely understood or expressed as clearly as this:

'I always manage to a greater or lesser degree to control my feelings for certain periods and then I begin to fall apart and the anticipated 'explosion' makes me full of anxiety and I begin to panic. The more I seem to be falling to pieces the more I desperately try to appear calm and normal and therefore remain silent. I did once foolishly try to explain to a doctor my feelings, but he said it is just my temperament and that I would have to learn to live with it, and if it really is bad sometimes to take a course of tranquillizers! One should test one's fears. I agree – if one can understand the fear. For example, if I am to start a new evening class I spend the time from enrolment night to the first night of class in thinking up all the reasons why I don't really want to go, but I can understand that it is only a fear of meeting new people and I test the fear and go, and usually end up after two or three weeks by knowing and being friendly with everyone there. What I don't understand, and therefore cannot test, is the basic fear and the basic insecurity. John wants us to be married this year, but I cannot do that without getting into a terrible flap (not about all the arrangements, because I have a meticulous and calm mind for organization) but because I feel I am then going to be completely on my own (of course I know in actual fact this is not so!), more accessible to hurt (I can't explain the reason for this) and, the most important feeling, once 'found out' I will be abandoned. What seems incomprehensible to me is that I know this is a lot of rubbish but I still cannot dispel the feeling about it. My feelings about a husband are that I want him to wrap me up in cotton wool, protect me from every unpleasant thing in life and not to hurt me. My reason tells me that I want to be as adult as him and to share with him all life's ups and downs. I have asked myself whether I really need anyone else. If I really am self-sufficient (and who is?) I wouldn't be so dreadfully upset at the fact that I cannot get close to someone else. John says that it doesn't really matter if the love only comes from him (in practice I believe he would be just as unhappy as anyone else if love could not be shown to him since we all need it) but it matters terribly to me. I want to be able to show and give love as well as to receive it. Before courting him I had always liked John, and I used to think what a wonderful husband he would be for somebody – whenever I thought like this about a boy it was always a wonderful husband for somebody else, never for me. I was never self-pitying about it; to me it was just a fact. When John asked me to marry him I thought he was playing a cruel joke on me, and although I liked him in return I never at any time made the first attempt at any demonstrations of love because I still feel unsure of the fact that he really wanted me. I watched him like a hawk for months in case my original surmise was after all true. Although I now know that it isn't true, the insecure feelings are still there. (I wish we were all born without feelings and were all cold, hard, matter-of-fact robots!).'

The problems highlighted in this personal history are the marked fear of being found unacceptable and her inability to express and return love to her fiancé. Some modifications of these problems are essential before the close and lasting relationship necessary for marriage is formed, which would otherwise run the risk of breaking down early on in its life. These and other emotional problems indicate clearly why difficulties in the engagement period should be taken seriously and evaluated psychologically before marriage is proceeded with.

The available research so far has pinpointed these danger signals and it is up to everyone concerned with education for marriage to take heed and accept their significance. Home, school and counselling services must co-ordinate their efforts to inform, educate and assist in every possible way so that marriages are not started under obvious handicaps.

Ultimately prevention must be directed towards an adequate and effective preparation for marriage. In its early stages this education was narrowly construed as sexual education, particularly sexual biology. Knowing how the body functions and the way the sexual exchange can be fully enjoyed are certainly important and both information and instruction have been long overdue. A later development has been the running of courses dealing with some of the realities facing the newly married. Desirable as both of these are, they cannot be substitutes for the continuous preparation of children at home and at school. It is at home above all that children will experience their first and most vital contact with marriage in the relationship of the parents. What they see, experience and feel about this exchange will influence their own potential roles and expectations. It is the marriage of the parents that will give meaning and shape to the goals of their own future marriage, hence the vital importance of preventing marital disharmony between the parents.

It is also during childhood that the vital developments in personality will take place. During these years the certainty of being wanted and the feeling of being acceptable and desirable for one's own sake will be developed. Concurrently personal independence and security in one's identity will be established. In so far as these characteristics make a marital relationship possible, then, far-fetched as it may appear, prevention of marital breakdown is primarily the work of appropriate psychological safeguards in the development of the personality. Society has slowly to absorb and implement the many insights acquired over three quarters of a century, from various psychological advances. The need for security, certainty in affection, the promotion of a sufficient and reliable identity and the elimination of anxieties and uncertainties about the personal value of the individual are some of the major items which all agree are vital. Inadequacies in these areas are the result of adverse factors in heredity and environment but the former is subject to modification through the positive influence of the latter.

Society has to take short- and long-term measures to safeguard marriage. The former involve recognizing warning signals and providing effective pre- and post-marital counselling. The latter concerns the correct upbringing of children, a difficult and challenging task, but one that is likely to prove in the long run the best safeguard against marital breakdown.

SIXTEEN

RECONCILIATION

THERE have been no large-scale detailed studies on the subject of marital therapy, so that there is little evidence on which to answer such fundamental questions as who seeks it, from whom, and what is the long-term outcome. Information is available about the numbers seeking help. For example in 1963, 41,815 cases were brought to the notice of the probation service. In 1964 the National Marriage Guidance Council gave 57,040 interviews, the Catholic Marriage Advisory Council 17,905, and the Family Discussion Bureau just over 3,500. These numbers do not include the families helped by the Family Welfare Association and, of course, thousands of families in the psychiatric clinics. It is clear that there are scores of thousands of people seeking help.[88]

The Morton Commission (Royal Commission on Marriage and Divorce 1951–55) recommended an early beginning, a positive impulse on one side at least, and complete assurance that nothing said to a counsellor will ever be disclosed without the consent of the person concerned, as some of the necessary prerequisites for successful reconciliation.[89]

Some motivation is undoubtedly necessary for, if one or both partners are adamant against reconciliation, there is nothing further that can be done. In this context an early start is helpful since attitudes have not hardened, and hope is still present. On the other hand, an early attempt may be handicapped not by the willingness of the couple but by the absence of a sufficient degree of maturity to appreciate the issues involved or the absence of the capacity to change. For such a marriage an early attempt to effect reconciliation may not actually save it but it can appraise the couple of the real situation, thus preventing procreation and the complications that this development could create in the future.

Assuming then a sufficiently positive motivation and the

right conditions of professional trust, what does reconciliation involve? It assumes that the needs, desires and hopes that brought the couple together can be fulfilled to a minimum degree of mutual satisfaction, provided that the appropriate assistance is given. Implicit in this formulation is the belief that each partner has the necessary capacities and is capable of developing them. It can be seen immediately that an adequate training is absolutely necessary for this work, so that these evaluations are based as far as possible on objective and reliable criteria rather than on the arbitrary and subjective views of the individual counsellor.

After such initial evaluation two separate courses of action are available either or both of which are pursued depending on circumstances. First is the offering of immediate and constructive assistance on practical matters. Secondly, there is the non-judgemental attention with which people are helped to clarify within themselves the significant issues. It is now widely recognized than in marital counselling as in every other form of counselling involving inter-personal relationships, feelings and emotions are the principal experiences which need recognition, ventilation and understanding.

The complete absence of suitable accommodation, work, money or the presence of interfering relatives and/or friends are matters which engage immediate attention and, whenever possible, should be rectified. Some couples will be sufficiently relieved by these environmental changes to allow them to apply themselves successfully to their personal problems. Similarly, ill health, physical or psychological, needs remedying. It is not possible to engage in effective reconciliation in the presence of pain, excessive fatigue, insomnia, marked anxiety and/or depression. It is perfectly true that often these symptoms are stress manifestations of the underlying conflict but this is initially obvious to the adviser only. Even when this insight is acquired by clients, they may need sufficient medical relief with drugs to allow them to concentrate on their inter-personal tensions.

Another group of initial difficulties arises from differences in religion, race, social class and social status, particularly if the latter rises in the course of the marriage through the promotion of one or the other spouse, usually the husband. Such an advance may take one partner into circles beyond the talent and outlook of the other, for whom the new activity becomes a cumbersome embarrassment. Similarly without a common faith, and common values, aims, ideals and social customs, some of the most powerful means of cementing a marital bond are lacking.

As soon as possible in every case of reconciliation an evaluation has to be made of the primary and secondary causes responsible for the difficulties. Generally speaking the couple will emphasize the material deprivation, social differences, ill health and unpleasant characteristics of the offending partner. It is the task of the counsellor to assist in the removal of any obvious physical and social liabilities by suggesting the appropriate source of help, and then to concentrate on what is by common consent the root of marital disharmony, namely personality conflicts.

To achieve this, sympathy, empathy and infinite patience are the essential ingredients without which counselling is unlikely to succeed. Clients respond to men and women from whom they receive a sympathetic understanding. A warm, friendly approach is helped by the non-judgemental character of the exchange. The counsellor is there to listen, not to pass judgement, criticize or offer his own particular brand of solutions. The listening needs more than sympathy, it requires empathy. Counsellors must be able to communicate to the client that they are able to understand, if possible feel and certainly accept unconditionally their predicament. When thus in accord, a great deal of patience is needed to sustain the client while painful changes are taking place.

These changes involve making the client see that the 'obvious' material and social 'causes' are not, in the vast majority of cases, the root of the problem. It is emotional difficulties and feelings that have to be recognized, acknowledged and slowly changed. Self-rejection needs to be modified sufficiently to accept the care and love of others. Similarly emotional growth of sufficient degree needs to be gained to reduce dependence and achieve a moderate degree of self-reliance. The increase of self-reliance and the diminution of self-rejection will, in turn, reduce the frustration and hostility experienced in the apparent failure of the partner to meet these immature requirements.

The question is often asked why it is necessary to have a counsellor or therapist at all. As soon as insight is achieved about the nature of the difficulty, surely, it is claimed, it should be possible to change it through unaided personal effort. This enquiry is made particularly by people of high intelligence for whom all problems are ultimately a matter of common sense demanding only intellectual solutions. It is not sufficiently realized that emotional difficulties are intimately related to previous unsatisfactory human relationships and their solution needs the presence of another human being. Counselling and psychotherapy provide the other human presence, sufficiently trained, dedicated and free of personal difficulties, to provide the client with a second opportunity to work out problems which may have remained ever since the first encounter with the parents. Effective counselling provides a fresh opportunity through which clients can discover their own value, their potential and their capacity to give themselves. The counsellor is the human agent who helps to discover their worth and accepts them as people worthy of love. A successful marriage, of course, achieves precisely this mutual acknowledgement and acceptance, which in turn promotes further personal growth. This is a positive and creative circle as compared to the vicious and destructive one caused by marital disharmony.

A counsellor may work with an individual client but increasingly marital therapy is moving in the direction of assisting the spouses to act as therapists to one another by seeing them together. This can be done by meeting the couple alone or in a group with several other couples. The group atmosphere assists to remove misunderstandings, brings out quickly the fact that problems do not lie exclusively with one or the other and allows the establishment of a quick *rapport* in those areas where urgent assistance is needed.

While ideally both partners should be involved in the work of repairing and reconstructing their relationship, this is not always possible. The reasons for this are many. In a relationship of two vulnerable personalities the recognition of the need to seek help requires a certain amount of courage and strength to sustain the person in the discoveries and revelations regarding themselves. The very act of seeking help appears to be an admission of failure which few people find it easy to make. The fact that one spouse takes this step does not necessarily mean that the other is prepared to face or is capable of facing his or her own difficulties and shortcomings. In fact he may exploit to the maximum the difficulties of the other spouse on whom the whole blame is laid. And, often enough, the spouse who seeks advice hopes that marital success will be achieved merely through changes solely in themselves. This very rarely succeeds because, in the course of examining the marriage, the shortcomings of the other partner will become increasingly obvious. Even if, therefore, one partner is prepared to take the initiative, either independently or through pressure, very soon the essential contribution of the other will become clear. At this stage the spouse who initially sought help may either refuse to continue without the cooperation of the other person or he may gradually manage to convince his partner of the need to seek help as well. An alternative outcome is the situation where the persistent refusal of one spouse to seek help promotes the maturation and strengthening of the other, who is helped to the point where he or she can accept and tolerate the resistant spouse, with all their limitations.

One of the constant dangers of marital therapy is that therapeutic changes in one person will change the delicate balance holding the partners together causing the other partner to suffer a complete breakdown. This may take place in a situation of marked competition between the spouses in which the partnership is preserved by the ability of each to demonstrate to the other their failures and in this way maintain an image of adequacy about themselves. Furthermore, the presence of these weaknesses provides a safety valve by means of which anger and resentment can be rationally directed towards one another without a sense of injustice or feelings of guilt being experienced. The subtle change of one partner in the absence of a similar change in the other, places the person with the improvement in an immediate advantage, exposing the other to the full anxieties of his own problems and inadequacies. If this proves too much, then the result is a complete breakdown. Similarly the husband or wife who urges their spouse to seek aid may find when this is received that, as a result of this help, the balance is changed to their own disadvantage and the initial encouragement is turned into a series of oppositions and obstacles placed in the way of further change. An expression of this opposition may be seen in the efforts of the uninvolved spouse either to stop treatment altogether or to provoke a return to old habits in order to return to the previous equilibrium, however unsatisfactory this may have been.

Marriage therapy thus involves total help. Social, material and health problems should each receive adequate and effective attention clearing the way for the changes in personal traits which will allow a sufficient degree of fusion and integration matching the minimal requirements and capacities of the partners.

Marital counselling is available through the organizations listed below.

(A) PROBATION OFFICERS

The probation service deals probably numerically with the greatest number of cases. Couples approach probation officers voluntarily or find their way into their care via the courts.

(B) THREE VOLUNTARY ORGANIZATIONS RECOGNIZED BY THE HOME OFFICE WHO ARE IN RECEIPT OF GRANTS FROM THE EXCHEQUER

These are the *National Marriage Guidance Council*, which has some 120 counselling centres staffed by nearly 1,000 voluntary counsellors, selected and trained by the national body. *The Catholic Marriage Advisory Council* has currently nearly seventy centres served by 500 counsellors. *The Family Dis-*

cussion Bureau, which was set up in 1948 is now part of the Tavistock Institute of Human Relations. It has three aims:

i. To provide a service for people seeking help with marriage problems.

ii To devise techniques appropriate to such a service, and evolve a method of training caseworkers.

iii. To find out something about problems of inter-personal relationships as they reveal themselves in marital difficulties.

In nearly twenty years of its work this bureau has distinguished itself by its help to marriages in need, its scientific contributions and the training of social workers and general practitioners. It remains one of the few centres offering specialized facilities for these types of problems, emphasizing in its work the psycho-analytic principles of personality interaction. Some of its early results were published in a book called *Social Casework in Marital Problems*[90] and later in *Marriage, Studies in Emotional Conflict and Growth.*[91] In addition to the Family Discussion Bureau, the Marital Unit exists at the Tavistock Clinic. This unit was established through the initiative of Dr H. V. Dicks who in his recent book[92] summarizes the work carried out in the unit. The advances in our understanding of marital pathology owe a great deal to this research and it is a pleasure to record this here.

(C) FAMILY SERVICE UNITS

This too is a voluntary organization which undertakes to offer help to families, particularly those in severe social distress. The workers may live with these families and combine material assistance with marital counselling.

(D) THE PSYCHIATRIC SERVICES IN THE HEALTH SERVICE

It is difficult to estimate the work that is being done in this field under the umbrella of the psychiatric services. Marital disharmony and pending dissolutions are recurrent features of the marriages of the patients who reach the psychiatrist. The scope of the therapy depends on the resources available and the special interest of individual psychiatrists. Frequently marital therapy is carried out by psychiatric social workers who often achieve remarkable results in spite of the fact that this aspect of their work has to continue in the midst of innumerable other urgent demands.

Thus the bulk of the work of reconciliation is carried out by marriage counsellors, probation officers and other social agencies. These organizations have strict criteria for selection and the future counsellors undergo a training course prior to beginning counselling. This arrangement raises some major issues. Is the counselling service as at present instituted sufficient in numbers, is it effectively organized and sufficiently backed by expert knowledge and research work?

The Morton Commission recommended future developments through existing agencies. There is a great deal to be said for this except that in addition local authorities should extend their responsibilities well beyond the facilities currently offered. There is need for a specific marriage counselling service separate from probation work, concerned exclusively with the couple and their children. Such a service would have specific advantages over the present probation service and the marriage counselling organizations.

Probation officers have a great deal of other work to do, they are not primarily concerned with marriage as such, and are associated in the eyes of the public with the rehabilitation of offenders. All this diminishes in no way the invaluable work they do in marriage cases but the fact remains that this is not the principal work for which they were trained. The time is now appropriate for a separate marriage counselling service organized by the local authority, with its own distinctive characteristics.

As far as the voluntary organizations are concerned they still have a vital contribution to make through their experience and their specific religious affiliation. They suffer, however, from the handicap which so many other organizations experience, namely, they are not evenly used by all socio-economic groups. There is a tendency for the upper socio-economic groups to make greater use of these voluntary facilities.

An extension of marriage counselling by local authorities raises thorny issues such as the availability of trained personnel, the country's capacities for training such personnel and the availability of research on marital breakdown. The answer to all these points and particularly to the last one leaves a great deal to be desired. The only professionally trained workers in marital work are social workers and a few doctors and even then marriage is not their exclusive preoccupation. Marriage counsellors for whom marriage *is* their exclusive work *do not* receive a professional training although of course individuals already professionally trained do undertake voluntary counselling. *This dilemma can only be resolved in my opinion by the training of professional social workers to be concerned entirely with marriage and who can undertake this work on behalf of the local authority, the courts and the voluntary organizations.*

The need for research in this field is urgent and vital but it receives very little specific attention in this country. Research on marriage presents a major challenge because of the multiplicity of sociological and psychological factors involved. Below are outlined some of the major issues that have to be tackled.

(A) SOCIOLOGICAL

a. Further epidemiological studies accurately defining subgroups which carry high risks of marital breakdown with precise identification of the social and psychological difficulties and with particular emphasis on the first five years of marriage.

b. Sociological research has connected divorce with such factors as youthfulness, youthfulness and pre-marital pregnancy, pre-marital pregnancy and hasty marriages. But not all these couples come to grief. There is need for combined psycho-social studies to clarify further the specific factors responsible for the breakdown.

c. Sociological studies in the United States have associated divorce with non-Church weddings and low socio-economic position. These findings have not been confirmed in Great Britain. Further research is required, preferably combined psycho-social studies.

d. The success or failure of re-marriages and the factors responsible for either result.

Impact on children:

i. Too little is known of the damage that children suffer in divorced homes as compared to the non-divorced but disturbed households.

ii. The vulnerability of the child in relation to age.

iii. The vulnerability of the child in relation to sex.

iv. The vulnerability of the child in relation to the reconstruction of its family life in a further marriage.

(B) CLINICAL

a. Factors operating in spouse selection in terms of personality characteristics.

b. Perhaps one of the major challenges to marital research is the change in personality, personal needs and expectations with age during different phases of the family cycle.

c. The pathology of psychological interaction with particular attention to the personality traits of (i) dependence (ii) self rejection (iii) insecurity.

d. The development of effective and acceptable means of birth control and the means of reaching those families which are in special need.

e. Detailed psychological examination of non-consummation and the appropriate means of helping it.

f. Information is needed to relate the marital problem to the correct agency for help. Some marriages will respond to the help of a marriage council, others to the probation service, and so on. Others need more detailed psychological help. Appropriate evaluation and direction will eliminate a lot of wasted and unrewarding effort.

g. Examination of post-puerperal syndromes.

(C) THERAPY

Precise evaluation of therapy in terms of

i. type

ii. duration

iii. the age, social class and background of those seeking help.

iv. Period of marriage prior to the seeking of help.

(D) EDUCATIONAL

Education for marriage begins at home, continues at school and is particularly important just before and immediately after marriage. Research is needed to find out the best way of carrying out this educational programme.

There can be little doubt that what is urgently needed is the setting up of a few selected research units, adequately financed and staffed by sociologists, psychologists and psychiatrists, to further knowledge and new techniques, offering the widest and most effective help for those who seek it. The work of marriage counsellors, probation officers and others is a story of hard effort battling with complex and, at times, incomprehensible and impossible problems. These workers are often criticized for their naivety and lack of professional expertise. Sometimes these criticisms are justified but what is frequently forgotten is the appalling lack of support they receive. There is little doubt that the work of marriage reconciliation would become easier with appropriate help from research workers and specialists in this field.

SEVENTEEN

THE LAW

IF neither prevention nor reconciliation will solve the fate of a particular marriage there is one other radical solution, namely relief from the courts through divorce.

In England and Wales the 1857 Matrimonial Causes Act established the right of civil divorce. Until 1857 divorce could only be obtained by a series of complicated steps in which the petitioner had first to go to the civil court to claim damages from the offender, then to an ecclesiastical court to prove the matrimonial offence and finally to Parliament for a private act. It is estimated that the cost for all this was of the order of £700–£800. It is not, therefore, surprising to find that between 1715 and 1852, a period of nearly one and a half centuries, only 244 divorces were granted. The 1857 Act simplified the procedure considerably by allowing the petitioner to sue for divorce throughout in one court, now established in one special division of the High Court. The decrease in cost was considerable, even though reduced in undefended cases to an estimated sum of about £50. The financial burden, still high for the vast majority of people, was further reduced by financial assistance through government action in 1914 and more extensively in the Legal Aid and Advice Act of 1949.

With the principle of civil divorce established, and the financial burden reduced to proportions debarring few from having access to it, there remained the question of the grounds for obtaining it. This has been the source of more than one Royal Commission and a great deal of controversy. The 1857 Act continued to distinguish between annulment and divorce. Annulment was granted if a marriage was within the prohibited degree of affinity or consanguinity, or if mental or physical incapacity led to non-consummation, and bigamy. Divorce was allowed initially for the wife's adultery alone if the husband was the petitioner and for the husband's adultery, aggravated by either cruelty or desertion on his part, if the petitioner was the wife. This glaring example of discrimination between the sexes was removed by the 1923 Matrimonial Causes Act which allowed wives to petition on similar grounds as the husband, namely for adultery alone. Sir Alan Herbert's Matrimonial Causes Act of 1937 provided a further major change in the law, allowing dissolution not only on the grounds of adultery but also of desertion, cruelty, and prolonged incurable insanity. Apart from insanity, these are all based on an uninterrupted legal principle of matrimonial offence whereby dissolution is obtained if one of the spouses can be shown to have violated the contract by action or behaviour inconsistent with the contractual nature of marriage, involving unilateral responsibility and guilt for the breakdown. As Rowntree and Carrier [3] pointed out 'incompatibility of temper', 'mutual consent', or 'irretrievable breakdown of marriage', that is mutual recognition of marital failure, although recommended as grounds for dissolution from as far back as 1853 to as recently as 1956, have not yet been accepted by any government in this country.

The classic definition of marriage in English law is that of Lord Penzance in Hyde & Hyde in which he stated: 'I conceive that marriage, as understood in Christendom may.... be defined as the voluntary union of one man and one woman to the exclusion of all others.' [93] Marriage is thus voluntary, lifelong and monogamous and in English law it is effected by a contract whereby a man and woman enter into a legal relationship with each other which creates and imposes mutual rights and obligations. The violation of this contract constitutes the matrimonial offence which remains up to the present the sole ground for divorce. Section 1 of the Matrimonial Causes Act 1965 lists four grounds (adultery, desertion, cruelty and incurable unsoundness of mind) in which either party may petition for divorce and three (rape, sodomy and bestiality) in which a wife alone may petition.[94]

The law on divorce is currently under critical re-examination in this country with a view to extending the grounds on which divorce will be obtainable and, even more fundamentally, to re-evaluating whether the matrimonial offence is the appropriate concept on which to base the termination of marriage. At the time when this book was going to press Mr William Wilson's bill for divorce on the grounds of mutual consent and the breakdown of marriage was about to be presented to Parliament. Whatever the outcome it is worth examining briefly the present position. The branding of one party as the offender has indisputable legal advantages in that the violation of the contract can be demonstrated, guilt placed on the appropriate partner and justice done to the offended party. Unfortunately in the overwhelming number of cases this view is an utter denial of the truth. The man or woman who commits adultery, is cruel or deserts their partner has certainly offended against the other party. But who is to assess the offence of the so-called innocent party and their failure or incapacity to meet the minimum needs of the offending partner? By condemning the overt behaviour of one, particularly in cases of adultery, the grave risk is run of ignoring the failure, deliberate or otherwise, of the partner who provoked the offence. Provocation is certainly taken into account in the courts, but decisive and clear-cut provocation is blurred by the subtleties of human behaviour. People provoke without knowing that this is happening, damage when they intend to protect, destroy when they seek to salvage, consciously seek friendship while unconsciously they mete out anger, punishment and revenge. No court can be expected to evaluate such *minutiae* of human conduct but no society should delude itself that the discovery of legal guilt exonerates the innocent party from responsibility.

It can be argued that the law recognizes these limitations and that the matrimonial offence, with all its restrictions, provides an effective and reliable tool to work with. There are undoubtedly practical advantages in this view but in my opinion the law reflects an attitude which is no longer compatible with the essence of marriage. The contractual nature of marriage has a long and distinguished history from the period of Roman jurisprudence, through centuries of Canon Law up to the present. The indisputable fact remains that while it is the voluntary, lifelong and monogamous commitment which initiates marriage, its essence is undoubtedly the ability of the couple to translate these vows into a *viable relationship.*[95] Marriage is a commitment to a physical, emotional, social and spiritual relationship. The civil law must move from the present concept of matrimonial offence in the direction of establishing and safeguarding the essential elements of a viable relationship. When a court is satisfied that these elements never existed or have ceased to exist, a marriage may be considered non-existent or terminated.

The granting of civil divorces is infinitely better suited to the recognition by the courts of a total cessation of a relationship. The law of divorce would move in the direction of pragmatism as well as safeguarding both parties, by encouraging second thoughts and a recourse to effective reconciliation whenever there is the slightest chance of this happening. The desire of the couple and of society is not for disruption but for an effective reconciliation, if this is at all possible. This is currently handicapped by the marked lack of knowledge of what is possible in reconciliation. In order to assist the courts, it is essential that their work of evaluating the viability of a marriage is assisted by the type of social worker referred to in the previous chapter, trained and entirely devoted to marital work, and assisted, whenever necessary, by the appropriate medical experts. The research already referred to will become increasingly important and must receive the support of research funds from local authorities and the government.

The notion of marital breakdown was advanced by Lord Walker[96] in a separate document of the Royal Commission on Marriage and Divorce which reported in 1955 and has been most ably discussed in the report of a group appointed by the Archbishop of Canterbury called 'Putting Asunder', giving, in 1966, the recommendations of the Church of England.[88] While the law must change to meet the requirements of a pluralistic society, there is bound to be inevitable anxiety in Christian circles about any change or extension of divorce procedure. How would the principle of marital breakdown fit in with the traditions of canonical jurisprudence?

Ever since the Old Testament, marriage has been depicted as a relationship between God and His people and St Paul reaffirms Christian marriage as a union of two in one between husband and wife with a relationship that 'parallels, imitates and participates in, so far as is possible, the closeness and love exchanged between Christ and his bride, the Church'.[97] Marriage seen as a relationship fits in perfectly with Christian teaching. The spiritual and physical aspects of this relationship have already received attention from Christian tradition. St Paul himself, in the famous Pauline privilege, allowed dissolution and remarriage in the case of two non-baptized persons, one of whom became baptized but was hindered by the partner in the fulfilling of their Christian obligations, thus extolling the importance of a viable spiritual relationship. Dissolution with remarriage is also allowed in cases of non-consummation, adding to the spiritual relationship the importance of the physical one. To these established physical and spiritual factors is now added perhaps the single most important aspect, namely the ability of the couple to form an *emotional* relationship. Psychological advances in the last hundred years have slowly paved the way for a much greater understanding of the psychological factors which render a relationship impossible. From the Christian point of view marital breakdown may be, and indeed is, seen as an extension of nullity whereby one or both partners who make lifelong vows to love one another find in practice that they are incapable of actualizing in the relationship the initial commitment they have undertaken.

When is a marriage irretrievably broken? Lord Walker's definition is 'Where the facts and circumstances affecting the lives of the parties adversely to one another are such as to make it improbable that an ordinary husband and wife would ever resume cohabitation.'[98] The advantages of this definition are many. It does not make divorce necessary on grounds of a single or multiple acts of adultery, desertion or cruelty as long as they do not destroy the capacity and desire of a couple to overcome their difficulties and succeed in the future. Cohabitation depends on the *desire* and the *capacity* of a couple to continue a marital relationship.

If the law changes completely towards the principle of marital breakdown, is this likely to encourage a further increase of divorce? Everyone genuinely concerned with the stability of marriage must ask this question constantly. The court is the ultimate deterrent to irresponsible, hasty, unwarranted dissolutions and has a decisive responsibility in preventing these. Its influence, of course, depends on the view taken of the natural history of marital breakdown. The overwhelming majority of marriages start with a genuine desire, hope and promise that the goals and aspirations of the partners will be achieved. Between eighty and ninety per cent of the participants achieve a variable degree of success and the others persevere for a long time to avoid the human predicament aptly summarized by one eminent psychiatrist in these words: 'For there can be no question that divorce is always a tragedy no matter how civilized the handling of it; always a confession of human failure, even when it is the sorry better of sorry alternatives.'[37] Few couples reach the divorce courts without suffering a great deal and trying very hard to preserve a union in which they have invested their highest hopes and expectations. The principle of marital breakdown allows the most civilized answer which faces reality without indicting and apportioning guilt, an unnecessary cruelty of present procedure. It also permits the court to carry out a final evaluation which still allows for reconciliation whenever this is at all possible.

*

NOTE. The Divorce Reform Act 1969 came into force in January 1971, making irretrievable breakdown the sole grounds for dissolution of marriage.

EIGHTEEN

MARITAL BREAKDOWN AND THE FUTURE

IN this last chapter no attempt will be made to predict the future trends in marital breakdown. There is not enough accurate and reliable information to do this. Instead, however, an assessment will be made of the significance and implications of the increased incidence of breakdown in this century. Goode[99] has collected data from official sources from various countries showing the rising incidence of divorce.

Table 6

Divorce rates in selected western countries

	Number of divorces per 1,000 marriages	
	1910	1956
Country		
United States	87·4	246·2
Germany	30·2	89·2
England & Wales	2·2 (1911)	74·4
Australia	12·9	90·4
France	46·3	100·5
Sweden	18·4	175·4

These figures, which speak for themselves, come from countries that allow divorce. Others, such as Spain, Italy and Ireland, allow only legal separations without the right of re-marriage. The fact that these predominantly Catholic countries do not allow divorce does not of course stop marital breakdown.

This is clearly demonstrated by the large number of Irish people in Britain. There is no evidence that they exhibit more or less marital instability than other people. When their marriage breaks down, those who continue to practise their faith separate, as they would have done at home, and those ceasing to do so, make use of divorce and remarry. Unfortunately the introduction of divorce has led to some futile controversies between those who see in its presence the cause of marital breakdown, and the opponents, who hail it as the only solution. These two forces represent in our society today an apparently inevitable opposition. One group mobilizes all the traditional arguments as to the need to preserve the stability of marriage and is against any further loosening of the marital bond by easier divorce; the other considers the right and freedom of the individual to seek happiness unhampered as the most important objective, to be pursued with remorseless zeal, despite opposition from the state and the churches.

Represented and repeatedly discussed in and out of Parliament in this way, as a battle between freedom and liberalism and the forces of conservatism, it appears clear cut and simple. And yet no one working with the couples themselves would recognize the problem in such clearly defined terms. On the contrary, one finds oneself with human beings in the grips of an acute and bewildering catastrophe threatening the most important experience of their lives. Only too frequently there are children who are torn by conflicting emotions and feelings, hopelessly at the mercy of the insecurity of their position. On the one hand, those who place the happiness of the individual uppermost tend to exaggerate the usefulness of divorce as a suitable means of achieving this. On the other, those who see the breakdown of marriage as a massive movement towards irresponsibility and pleasure-seeking have rarely listened to, or participated in, the suffering and unhappiness which have made individuals finally take the step of seeking warmth and reassurance from somebody else.

There is a great need for society to move away from this sterile battle between those who seek to preserve the *status quo* and those who seek a further extension of divorce. An infinitely more rewarding and pragmatic level of approach would be to discover, through research, what are the ingredients that *make a marriage viable at all and thus to separate the humanly possible from the impossible.*

Research along psychological and sociological lines would gradually clarify the basic question of when a marriage is a marriage, and effort could be concentrated on salvaging every marriage that is open to rescue work based on modern knowledge. Similarly, delineating the genuine human possibility of marriage will help the Christian Churches to accept the fact that when a marriage is only a marriage in name, then there is little point in defending the bond in the name of Christian teaching. Marriage, as recognized by society through its civil legislation and by the Christian Churches, is essentially a contract freely entered into by a man and a woman who give themselves to one another and undertake the duties, responsibilities and rights of that state. It has to be inquired whether some whose intelligence and intentions are on the surface apparently clear and unequivocal, are nevertheless, in the light of our increasing knowledge of the psychological aspects of the personality, incapable of giving adequate expression and meaning to their vows and verbal undertakings. The youthfulness of some marriages, the conscious and unconscious difficulties present in the personality, which may appear immediately or years later, have to be examined in the light of the fact that a marriage can only survive if it is a viable and effective relationship between two people. The core of severe marital difficulties is the disparity and inadequacy of two personalities effecting such a relationship, and therefore the question that has to be asked on all levels of pragmatism and morality is whether such marriages are in fact marriages at all.

The marriage of the psychopath (which terminates after a few days, weeks or months); of the dependent personality with the childlike need of a parental figure to support him; of the homosexual who seeks a cure through marriage: are these marriages in any sense at all except for the formality of the ceremony? To call them marriages is to delude everyone.

It is possible but of dubious validity to interpret the present incidence of divorce as an accurate indication of the minimum inevitable breakdown rate – now for the first time obvious – since the restraining forces of society and religion have been removed. The restraining forces of society have included disapproval, social isolation and hostility, inequality of the sexes, and at times active punitive retaliation. Religion has emphasized the threat of severe Divine retribution, which is now no longer accepted in these rigoristic terms. On the other hand – and this is where the uncertainty lies – the influence of education, prevention and reconciliation has just begun, and society has a long way to go to realize their significance, increase the available facilities, or fully utilize them.

Expert assistance through marriage counselling and psychiatry can help some – though not all – individuals to heal or ameliorate sufficiently their sense of personal inadequacy and frustration; to modify their needs and attune them to the capacities of the spouse; to see the partner in a new light, free from the prejudices of unwarranted phantasies and projections, and helping each other to mature to the point where infantile needs are left behind and replaced by a meaningful relationship based on reality. This is the goal of reconciliation.

But neither the psychiatrist nor the marriage counsellor should be expected to wear the mantle of the all-powerful healing magician who is able to remove all the ills of society. Advances in our understanding of man will certainly put at our disposal information which allows us to reach and handle effectively previously unrecognized and incompatible marital difficulties. But all marriages involve some striving and hardship, some effort to bring about a union out of two separate individuals and what no one can do is to make this passage painless. In fact, no amount of expert help can alter the social climate of the day, which determines the amount of pain and suffering that any person is willing to accept; nor can it set norms of expectations which the couple will seek in one another. Here the prevailing religious, ethical or philosophical orientations of the individuals are all-important. How much unhappiness one will allow in one's life depends up to a point on the view one has of the morality of divorce and the place of human suffering. Everybody would recognize that at one end of the scale no human progress can be made in the absence of struggle and personal suffering; on the other hand no one should be asked the impossible, at which point the demand ceases to be a meaningful human one. There would be a wide measure of agreement on these extremes. But it is the intervening situations which present the problems. How long do a couple persevere with a marriage which has a chance to work out in the fullness of time but will inevitably put a great deal of strain on them in the interval? Here Christianity – and most other ethical systems – which accept suffering as an intrinsic and significant part of living, contrast strongly with utilitarian philosophies which highlight the values of immediate satisfaction, happiness and the avoidance of suffering.

The advantages can be seen in the low overall incidence of divorce in couples practising and sharing the same faith (see Table 1, page 27). These figures have to be interpreted with caution. The absence of divorce or separation is not the final proof of a successful marriage. Christ's absolute prohibition of divorce can only be meaningful in the total context of His message of love. Whenever a Christian marriage is found in which the couple live under the same roof but in separate bedrooms, communicating through hostility and indifference and offering the children a pattern of antagonism and mutual destruction, the letter of the law may be complied with but the spirit of love is absent. Christ's commandment must become an imperative command to his followers, so as to initiate and contribute to a deeper understanding of the real meaning of marriage, not as an excuse for condemning others.

There are various urgent social problems confronting the world today. High among these are the removal of poverty and hunger, as well as the prevention and cure of disease. Our society has attained many of these objectives, and smaller but no less important ones are coming under scrutiny and receiving attention. The needs of the psychologically disturbed – those deprived in their youth or in old age – are claiming our attention, and small groups, such as the physically and mentally handicapped, are moving up in the priorities of our advanced society. A common difficulty runs through all these specialized challenges: the shortage of money, knowledge, and qualified people to deal with them.

Moving farther afield, there are a number of other social problems, such as juvenile delinquency, crime, alcoholism, sexual deviations and marital difficulties, which are just beginning to be recognized as challenges that must be faced and tackled with psychological and social means. These areas are more difficult to define because the issues are intimately associated with moral and social norms which in the past have elicited merely the demand for greater effort and discipline on the part of the participants. While society can deal with its offenders through prison or social ostracism, it is now increasingly acknowledged that neither prison nor any other form of punishment removes our collective or personal responsibility for them.

Marital disharmony is a responsibility that cannot be dealt with either through the rigours or the permissiveness of the law, because human happiness cannot be legislated for. Help for those who cannot find it for themselves has to come through the appropriate organizations and through men and women who are willing to help their neighbour in his plight.

REFERENCES

1. Maciver, R. M., and Page, C. H., *Society*, Macmillan, London, 1962
2. Pierce, R. M., *Sociological Review*, 1963, 11, p. 215
3. Rowntree, G., and Carrier, N., *Population Studies*, 1958, 11, p. 192
4. Rowntree, G., *Population Studies*, 1964, 28 No. 2, p. 147
5. Jacobson, P. H., *American Marriage and Divorce*, Holt, Rinehart & Winston, New York, 1959
6. Monahan, T. P., and Chancellor, L. G., *American Journal of Sociology*, 1955, 2
7. Hill, G. W., and Tarver, J. D., *Milbank Memorial Fund Quarterly*, 1952, 30, p. 5
8. Goode W. J., *After Divorce*, The Free Press, Glencoe, Illinois, 1956
9. Dahlberg, G., *Acta Genetica et Statistica*, Medica, 1948–51, 1–2, p. 319
10. Registrar-General, *Statistical Review of England and Wales for the year of 1963*, Part I, H.M. Stationery Office, London, 1965
11. Monahan, T. P., *American Sociological Review*, 1962, 27, p. 625
12. Clarke, A. C., *American Sociological Review*, 1952, 17, p. 17
13. Hollingshead, A. B., *American Sociological Review*, 1950, 15, p. 619
14. Glass, D. V. (ed), *Social Mobility and Marriage in Social Mobility in Britain*, Routledge & Kegan Paul, London, 1954.
15. Hillman, K. G., *Marital Instability and its Relation to Education, Income, and Occupation: an Analysis Based on Census Data in Selected Studies in Marriage and the Family*. Ed. Winch, R. F. McGinnis, R., Barringer, H. R., Holt, Rinehart & Winston, New York, 1962
16. Goode, W. J., *The Family*, Foundations of Modern Sociological Series, Prentice-Hall, New Jersey, 1964
17. Wallis, J. H., and Booker, H. S., *Marriage Counselling*, Routledge, Kegan & Paul, London, 1958, p. 131
18. Landis J. T., *Marriages of Mixed and Non-mixed Religious*

Faith in *Selected Studies in Marriage and the Family*, Holt, Rinehart & Winston, New York, 1962

19. Monahan, T. P., and Chancellor, L. E., *American Journal of Sociology*, 1955, 61, p. 233

20. Heiss, J. S., *Premarital Characteristics of the Religiously Inter-married in an Urban Area*, in *American Sociological Review*, 1960, 25 (1), p. 47

21. Wilner, D. M. (et al), *The Housing Environment and Family Life*, John Hopkins, Baltimore, 1962

22. Shaw, C. H., Wright C. H., *Lancet*, 1960, 1, p. 273

23. Terman, L. M., and Oden, M. H., *The Gifted Child grows up*, Stamford University Press, 1947

24. Burgess, E. W., and Wallin, P., *Engagement and Marriage*, Lippincott, 1953, p. 205

25. See reference 24, p. 195.

26. Strauss, A., *American Sociological Review*, 1946, 11, p. 554

27. See reference 24, p. 198

28. Slater E., and Woodside, M., *Patterns of Marriage*, Cassell, London, 1951

29. See reference 24, p. 199

30. See reference 24, p. 200

31. See reference 24, p. 209

32. Tharp, R. G., *Psychological Bulletin*, 1963, 60, p. 97

33. See reference 24, p. 529

34. Kreitman N., *British Journal of Psychiatry*, 1964, 110, No. 465, p. 159

35. Winch, R. F., Mate Selection, *A Study of Complementarity Needs*, Harper, New York, 1958

36. Wallin, P., *Journal of Social Psychology*, 1960, 51, p. 191

37. Kubie, L. S., *Psychoanalysis and Marriage* in *Neurotic Interaction in Marriage* ed. Eisenstein, V. W., Tavistock Publication, London, 1956

38. Kinsey, A. C. (et al), *Sexual Behaviour in Human Females*, Saunders, 1953, p. 377

39. Gebhard, P. H., *Journal of Social Issues*, 1966, 22, p. 88

40. See reference 38, p. 609

41. Hart, R. D. *British Medical Journal*, 1960, I, p. 1023

42. See reference 38, p. 380

43. Rainwater, L., and Weinstein, K. K., *And the Poor Get Children*, Quadrangle Books, Chicago, 1960

44. Rainwater, L., *Journal of Social Issues*, 1966, 22, p. 96

45. Bott, E., *Family and Social Network*, Tavistock Publications, London, 1957

46. See reference 38, p. 383

47. Gebhard, P. H., *Journal of Social Issues*, 1966, 22, p. 88

48. Clark A. L., and Wallin, P., *American Journal of Sociology*, 1965, 71, p. 187

49. Kinsey, A. C. (et. al), *Sexual Behaviour in the Human Male*, Saunders, Philadelphia and London, 1948, p. 236

50. East, W. N., *Society and the Criminal*, London, H.M.S.O., 1949

51 Blacker, C. P., *Lancet*, 1958, 1, p. 578

52. See reference 49, p. 651

53. Rosen, I., in *The Pathology and Treatment of Sexual Deviation*, Oxford University Press, London, 1964

54. Jacobson, P. H., *American Sociological Review*, 1950, 15, p. 235

55. Monahan, T. P., *American Sociological Review*, 1955, 20, p. 446

56. See reference 24, p. 721

57. Pierce, R. M., and Rowntree, G., Birth Control in Britain, *Population Studies*, 1961, 15, 1 and 2

58. Freedman, R., Whelpton, P. K., and Campbell, A. A., *Family Planning, Sterility and Population Growth*, McGraw Hill, New York, 1959

59. Taylor, W., *British Journal of Preventive and Social Medicine*, 1954, Vol. viii, p. 1

60. Warburton, D., and Fraser, C. F., *Human Genetics*, 1964, 16

61. See reference 28, p. 185

62. See reference 28, p. 198

63. Hare, E. H., and Shaw, G. K., *The British Journal of Psychiatry*, 1965, 111, No. 475, p. 461

64. Dominian, J., *Lancet*, 1963, 2, p. 293

65. Brown, G. W., (et. al), *Schizophrenia and Social Care*, Maudsley Monograph 17, 1966, Oxford University Press

66. Bardon, D., *Personal Communication*

67. Registrar-General, Statistical Review of England and Wales for the Year 1956, Part III, Table 38, p. 64

68. Monahan, T. P., The Changing Nature and Instability of Remarriages in *Selected Studies in Marriage and the Family*, Holt, Rinehart & Winston, New York, 1962

69. See reference 68, p. 633

70. *Deprivation of Maternal Care*, A Reassessment of its Effects, World Heath Organisation, Geneva, 1962

71. Otterström, E., *Acta Genetica et Statistica Medica*, 1952, 3, p. 72

72. Greer S., Gunn, J. C., Koller, K. M., *British Medical Journal*, 1966, 2, p. 1352

73. Greer, S., Gunn, J. C., *British Medical Journal*, 1966, 2, p. 1355

74. Greer, S., The British Journal of Psychiatry, 1966, 112, No. 486, p. 465

75. Jonsson, G., *Acta Psychiatrica Scandinavica*, 1967, Supplement 195, pp. 157–71

76. Despert, J. L., *Children of Divorce*, Doubleday & Co. Inc., Garden City, 1953

77. Landis, J. T., *Family Life Coordinator*, 1962, 11 (3), p. 61

78. See reference 24, p. 513

79. See reference 28, p. 47

80. Landis, J. T., *Social Forces*, 34 (3), p. 213

81. See reference 24, p. 514

82. Glick, P. C., *Stability of Marriage to Age at Marriage* in *Selected Studies in Marriage and the Family*, Holt, Rinehart & Winston, New York, 1962

83. Christensen, H. T., *Eugenics Quarterly*, 1963, 10 (3), p. 127

84. See reference 24, p. 548

85. Popenoe, P., *American Sociological Review*, 1938, 3

86. Kephart, W. M., *Sociology and Social Research*, 1952, 36 (5), p. 291

87. Davies, D. L., *British Journal of Preventive and Social Medicine*, 1956, 10, p. 123

88. *Putting Asunder*, S.P.C.K., 1966, London, pp. 150–54

89. *Report of Royal Commission on Marriage and Divorce*, 1951–5 (Cmd. 9678), para. 340

90. *Social Casework in Marital Problems*, Tavistock Publications, London, 1955

91. *Marriage Studies in Emotional Conflict and Growth*, Methuen, London, 1960

92. Dicks, H. V., *Marital Tensions*, Routledge, Kegan Paul, London, 1967

93. (f) 1866, L.R., I.P., and D., 130, 133 Bromley's Family Law, Butterworth, 1966

94. Section I, Matrimonial Causes Act, 1965

REFERENCES

95. Dominian, J., *Christian Marriage, The Challenge of Change*, Darton, Longman and Todd, London, 1967

96. See reference 89, p. 340 f.

97. See reference 95, p. 25

98. See reference 89, p. 340

99. See reference 16, p. 94

INDEX

MORE ABOUT PENGUINS AND PELICANS

Penguinews, which appears every month, contains details of all the new books issued by Penguins as they are published. From time to time it is supplemented by *Penguins in Print*, which is a complete list of all books published by Penguins which are in print. (There are well over four thousand of these.)

A specimen copy of *Penguinews* will be sent to you free on request, and you can become a subscriber for the price of the postage. For a year's issues (including the complete lists) please send 30p if you live in the United Kingdom, or 60p if you live elsewhere. Just write to Dept EP, Penguin Books Ltd, Harmondsworth, Middlesex, enclosing a cheque or postal order, and your name will be added to the mailing list.

Some other books published by Penguins are described on the following pages.

Note: *Penguinews* and *Penguins in Print* are not available in the U.S.A. or Canada

THE FAMILY AND MARRIAGE IN BRITAIN

Ronald Fletcher

Pulpits, rostrums, and the more deeply entrenched batteries of press and radio still resound with lamentations about the decay of family life in Britain. Our modern society, it is said, is in a condition of moral decline. Immorality, divorce, delinquency stalk the land . . . or so we are told.

Is there any truth in this murky picture? Or, on the contrary, do the facts quietly pronounce that the family is more stable and more secure today than ever before in our history? For history, when we survey all classes impartially, is largely a long tale of poverty, drudgery, desertion, and vagrancy.

In his systematic analysis of the subject, a sociologist discusses the extraordinary strength and resilience of the family group in the face of rapid and radical social changes and provides answers to questions which are often anxiously posed to us: Are married women working in industry neglecting their children? Has discipline within the family utterly disappeared or is today's relationship between parents and children a new and fuller one? Have teenagers really so much money to spend? And, even if this is so, is it so deplorable?

The book arrives at encouraging conclusions and discusses the basis for further improvements.

'. . . deserves to be compulsory reading in all schools and theological colleges' – *Times Literary Supplement*

'. . . the fullest outline there has yet been of the social history of the family in Britain' – Michael Young, *New Statesman*

THE CAPTIVE WIFE

CONFLICTS OF HOUSEBOUND MOTHERS

Hannah Gavron

Emancipated women today face a conflict of values: they are educated and socialized to expect the same things from life as men – yet as wives, and particularly as mothers, they are obliged to subordinate their more contemporary roles for the sake of their family.

Investigating this conflict Hannah Gavron has talked to a sample of middle- and working-class mothers and elicited answers to such questions as: How far do children tie mothers to the house and limit independence? Do mothers envisage a lifetime in the maternal role? How far is there real equality in marriage? And do mothers find their freedom restricted before they have really been free at all?

In this lucid and compassionate study Hannah Gavron describes the social and historical background of the captive wife, draws conclusions from her survey, and discusses possible routes of escape.

'A model of what a well-informed, humane and intelligent sociologist can do' – *New Society*

'A perceptive and telling account of the lives and difficulties of some young mothers' – *The Times Literary Supplement*

'In terms of human happiness it could be the most important book of 1966' – *Sunday Express*